FRIENDS AND FAMILY
BIPOLAR
SURVIVAL GUIDE

Surviving Today, Thriving Tomorrow

Debra and Mark Meehl

Meehl Foundation Press

Book Design: Paul McNeese
Optimum Performance Associates, Chandler, AZ
Cover Design and Art: Cari Buziak,
Aon Celtic Art, Toronto, Ontario, Canada

Meehl Foundation Press
242 East Vaughn Avenue
Gilbert, Arizona 85234
Email: meehlfou@meehlfoundation.org
Online at: http://www.meehlfoundation.org

Contents

- Join a Support Group
- Boundaries
- There are Few Absolutes
- Set Boundaries
- Codependence
- Do I Leave or Do I Stay?
- Taking Care of Yourself
- Connect With God, Spirit, Allah...
- Develop Your Own Support

- Protect Your Credit
- File For Disability As Soon As Possible
- VA Benefits
- Buy Term Insurance
- Set-up Trust Accounts
- Find Your Life Purpose
- Find the Right Job

- The Story We Tell Ourselves
- Mindfulness
- Learn to Meditate
- Affirmations
- Dialectical Behavioral Therapy (DBT)

Final Thoughts   153

Appendices   169

The Meehl Foundation

About the Authors

Coming Soon from the Meehl Foundation Press

Dedication

To our parents,
Buck and Suzi Joers,
Daniel Meehl,
Dick and Vanetta Warren,
and our adopted parents
Jan and Roger Woll,
and Paul Goff,
whose support and love is unfailing.

Acknowledgments

We wish to thank Carol Dagenet for her friendship, support, her invaluable help in editing this book, and her unwavering belief in the Meehl Foundation and us.

We truly appreciate the information and the support we have received from our doctor and therapist, Robert Zenner, M.D. and Linn Sharf, MSW, who together have kept Mark alive and Debra centered.

Mr. Steven Dietz, who saw us through crisis, provided accurate diagnosis, and walked with us as we began our journey to recovery.

Our gratitude also goes out to Paul McNeese of Optimum Performance Associates for helping us to produce this book for you.

Finally, the four women of wonder, masters who empower and hold me in the light while I spontaneously manifest my own desires.

Boundaries

No longer am I willing to lose my self-esteem, self-respect, my children's well-being, my job, home, possessions, safety, credit, sanity, or ***myself*** to preserve a relationship.

I am learning how to choose to give appropriately and with a sense of high self-esteem.

I am learning I can occasionally decide to give up something during conflict negotiations. But I'm no longer willing to *mindlessly* lose everything I have for the sake of relationships, appearance, or in the name of love.

Melody Beattie, from *Beyond Codendency*

Introduction

This is a *Survival Guide*. It is based on what we have learned and what we are doing, successfully, to deal with Bipolar Disorder and the impact it has had on our own family.

It is written for anyone attempting to live with a loved one who is bipolar. As often happens when you are struggling to come to grips with this disorder and the chaos it is causing in your life, you are looking for a road map, information and solutions. You need guidance and direction. You need this book.

We are not therapists nor are we doctors. We are a couple, like you, trying to deal with this illness on a daily basis. "If I had only known . . ." were our favorite words for a long time. Like many people trying to deal with this illness, we found plenty of information for the bipolar but no information on how families were to deal with this illness from a practical perspective. We were left with more questions than answers, more confusion than clarity, and more despair than hope.

For example:

♦ What did I need to have in my hand to file for disability for Mark?
♦ How did I need to go about digging us out of debt?
♦ What is the standard treatment protocol?
♦ How do I find the right therapist?
♦ The right medication doctor?
♦ The right communication skills?

We wanted answers - or at least someone who could point us in the right direction! There was no good information and definitely no manual on how to survive in the bipolar world. What little we did find was pessimistic and offered no help on how to keep our relationship together, how to survive and thrive in a bipolar relationship, and, most importantly, how to protect ourselves and our emotional well-being.

After struggling to find answers and following hours and hours of research and reading, we decided that no one should have to go through what we had experienced and that there had to be a positive source of information for the family, partners and friends of bipolars, which is why this Survival Guide came to be written.

Through our work in the Meehl Foundation, with doctors and therapists, and our daily experiences, we developed a list of things we have learned - facts, processes and procedures that no one told us about or warned us about or, in some cases, even knew about. As the list grew and as people continued to email us with questions and concerns, we realized that there were thousands of people like us who were saying, "If only I had known . . ."

In this manual, we will give you the best information we have found—clear directions and steps to follow and real life examples of this illness and its manifestations in our life. We have attempted to avoid repetition and long dissertations on what is common sense.

Some of the information is "state sensitive" and will require you to check with your state government for forms and information. Some resources will require you to go to specific websites to obtain particular information.

Some of the recommended readings have nothing to do with Bipolar Disorder but have been included because we are writing about your own mental health and emotional well-being, and these books are some of the best we have found for helping you reach those worthwhile, life-preserving goals. All the information is designed to give you back your life and help you survive in the bipolar world. We have paid particular attention to suggesting things that you can do that will help *right now!*

We believe that recovery, plus the ability to have and enjoy a "normal" life and loving relationships, lies in *mindfulness*, *emotional stability* and *personal spirituality*, combined with *medication and therapy* to reduce and overcome the effects of this illness.

Through mindfulness, we become aware of changes in behavior, mood and perception. This allows both the bipolar and the partner or family member to recognize the emotional changes and be alert to the "triggers" that often lead to manic and depressive episodes. By building a consciousness, an atmosphere of open communication, and a "partnership," the bipolar and non-bipolars in a family can work together to maintain a loving relationship, and they can create a mutually supportive environment without the roller coaster ride that usually characterizes Bipolar Disorder.

Emotional well-being is often overlooked or put on hold as people attempt to deal with the chaos that accompanies this illness. People simply fail to take care of themselves—and often their children—due to focusing so heavily on the bipolar. Emotional well-being is the indispensable cornerstone of keeping relationships and families together.

Regardless of your religious beliefs we recommend that you acknowledge the importance of spirituality. We believe that there are many paths to God and that a spiritual relationship is important in surviving with this illness. The bottom line for us is that you need someone on your side, and God is a wise companion of choice. We believe that spirituality in any form, when combined with mindfulness and emotional balance, helps keep you centered. Not only does spirituality help you and your bipolar partner stay centered and grounded, but also it can provide you with the intuitive "knowingness" and mental energy necessary to deal with this illness.

Finally, living in the bipolar world is not easy. Each day brings new challenges as well as positive steps towards recovery. Although there is no cure for Bipolar Disorder, there can be (and is) recovery through using the tools and information we have included in this Survival Guide. We hope that our work will give empowerment back to you and your bipolar loved one and that you will find comfort in the knowledge that you are not alone.

In the end, we believe that you can have a positive, mutually supportive, loving relationship with your bipolar and that together you can not only survive, you can actually *thrive*—as individuals, as a couple, and as a family.

Our Story—as told by Deb

The first time we—Debra and Mark—met was in 1982. At the time, we both had families and were raising small children. For the next couple of years, we maintained contact until finally the responsibilities of life and work took us in different directions. We lost touch, each of us becoming a pleasant memory in the other's mind. It would be fifteen years until fate—and our souls—brought us back together.

In the last year of the century, on a sunny summer morning, in Oregon, we once again found each other. The following months brought our two lives and two souls together. Passion, strength and desire joined with our commitment and belief in each other to form the foundation of our relationship. At the time, I was a respected college instructor and paramedic who taught Psychological Emergencies and Crisis Intervention and was an Advanced Crisis Debriefer. Mark had just closed his retail business and was working as a consultant and an independent contractor. As we settled into a life together and thought about the future and what we wanted for each other and our family, our days became filled with dreams and potential as our souls bonded. Soul mates, we were finally together.

By fall, we decided to move to Mazatlan, Mexico, along the western coast of the Mexican peninsula. It was a wonderful town and we spent hours walking the beaches and exploring our new home. It was a quiet and in many ways idyllic time for both of us and we let the world evolve around the outer edges of our life together. We had come to Mexico to find a place to open a Bed and Breakfast and spent afternoons looking at property and houses. Yet, nothing seemed just right. The following spring found us driving, trailer in tow, across the country to the other side and Cancun.

In Cancun, things began to slowly change for us. The environment was charged with the excitement and hustle and bustle of a major resort area. We traveled about to the tourist areas and attractions and continued to look for a place to put our Bed and Breakfast. We would still walk the beaches and play in the ocean, but we were becoming increasingly concerned about our son's education, making ends meet, and finding the right place to make and fulfill our dreams and aspirations. Finally, with the new school year approaching, we once again loaded the Jeep and the trailer and headed back to the US.

After a two-week stay in San Antonio, Texas, we headed to Idaho at the behest of Mark's brother and with the promise of employment and good schools. Unfortunately, the promises fell apart almost from the moment of our arrival, and Mark found himself under pressure to conform to his family's vision of what our life should look like. In their hard driving, results-oriented, wealth-driven world, we were seen as wanderers without direction or a plan. Although our critics made little or no effort to learn about and understand our plans and aspirations, they spent plenty of time determining the right course for our life. Finally, following a very unpleasant confrontation that took place exactly one week after our arrival, Mark and I once again loaded up the Jeep and we returned to Eugene, Oregon—closer to "our" family and friends—just as the economy careened into recession, soon forcing us to deplete our savings. We would spend the next five months in a green, lush environment, under gray and rainy skies, increasingly depressed and concerned about our situation and the lack of employment prospects. We needed a change, we needed jobs, and we needed sunshine.

The answer for us? Phoenix, Arizona. Warm, sunny, a booming economy—and 1,500 miles from the family—it seemed perfect. We quickly purchased a house, enrolled our son in school, and Mark returned to work with Fred Meyer Jewelers, for whom he had managed a store several years earlier. For the next three months, life was very good as we made new friends and basked in the warm sunshine. Work was going well, money was starting to come in again, and things were looking up. In May, we attended Mark's son's wedding and returned to Arizona to find Mark's job gone—without explanation, reason or cause. Mark slipped into depression within days.

Bipolar Disorder is a genetic illness, passing from one generation to the next, indiscriminately impacting the life of one family member while leaving the others unscathed. Often looking somewhat like alcoholism, drug addiction, gambling, employment instability or sexual indiscrimination—and punctuated with emotional highs and lows—Bipolar Disorder often hides behind life's ordinary experiences, emerging only when certain environmental "triggers" or "stressors" cause it to manifest itself.

We are convinced that the time period described above—nine short months, from the confrontation in Idaho to the termination in May—delivered to Mark an increasing number of triggers. These triggers, which were of varying severity and irregularly timed, ultimately allowed Mark's Bipolar Disorder to manifest itself, to crawl from under the protective blanket of his coping and survival skills and to fully display itself. Unable to recover from "the devastation" that occurred in Idaho, each succeeding trigger took on greater importance, and the emotional impact aggregated until Mark hit bottom—*months after it all began*.

As days became weeks and his depression incessantly increased, Mark's physician prescribed Zoloft, then Celexia, and then Effexor. Each would work for about three months, but eventually his body would adjust to the medication, and then Mark would once again be raging.

Even as he began attending real estate school in an attempt to realize his long time dream of selling real estate, he seemed to just be going through the motions. After having waited years for a combination of the right opportunity, the right market and having the time necessary to start a practice, real estate seemed, at that moment, to be the perfect pursuit. Yet something was clearly wrong. Mark gradually became distant, less and less communicative, unable to concentrate, and he was almost continually critical as he continued to battle his depression, which seemed to be deepening at times but was frequently followed by periods of optimism and heightened activity and energy.

By fall, Mark had changed real estate companies after having lost a sale to his supervisor, and as a consequence of the move he had to rebuild his clientele and business. Mark is intelligent, educated and driven. He started and managed businesses for years, yet here he was, suddenly and inexplicably struggling to get his feet underneath him. In addition, he had become disturbingly withdrawn. It was so bad at times that I wondered if Aliens had taken him away and left in his place someone who looked like Mark but was, in fact, a completely—and very unpleasantly—different person!

In an effort to find out what was wrong, I started to read about depression and related illnesses. In an effort to find support and answers, I began attending Al-Anon meetings and discussing what was happening at home. At the end of a meeting one night, a fellow group member suggested to me that Mark might be suffering not only from depression but might possibly be bipolar. With this new focus to investigate, I returned to the books and the Internet, looking for as much information as possible on this thing called Bipolar Disorder and its related illnesses.

Gone was the dream of opening a Bed and Breakfast as the future became increasingly clouded by the rapidly changing moods that Mark was experiencing. Everything seemed to be on hold while concerns for Mark's health, the environment at home, and the increasing instability of our relationship became paramount. It was clear that something was terribly wrong and we both needed professional help.

Enter the world of psychiatrists and therapists. After making several calls, we located a female doctor, an M.D. *and* a Ph.D., who was apparently at the top of her field and well respected. Almost immediately, she decided that Mark was seriously depressed, but, in her opinion, since there was no history of mental illness in his family he was most likely a victim of ADHD, Attention Deficit Hyperactivity Disorder, coupled with a case of situational depression. A drug called Ritalin would solve everything. She also recommended marriage counseling, since Mark had already decided that a divorce was the best solution. If only we would divorce, Mark believed, he would be fine and everything would again be "normal." Although "The Alien" would be happier, I wasn't so sure and was thus in no hurry to rush into divorce.

By spring, the doctor was regularly increasing the dosage of Ritalin as Mark's body adjusted to each dosage level and his mood swings heightened. His real estate efforts ground to a halt and he languished about the house, alternating between even deeper depression and briefly elevated moods, a warning sign of Bipolar Disorder. Mark would swing from extreme highs of obsessive-compulsive behavior accompanied by periods of raging, back down into severe depression.

In late May, Mark returned to Oregon to work on our property there and to prepare it for sale. What should have been a two-week project of cleanup and preparation became a six-week odyssey of obsessive-compulsively driven attempts at perfection, along with manic behavior. Friends and family there called to say that something was terribly wrong with Mark—but no one knew what it was.

On the 4th of July, I returned home in the afternoon and found Mark curled up in the fetal position on the bathroom floor, screaming that he just wanted to die. Quickly I called an old friend, a retired therapist, and he immediately brought Mark in for help. An hour later, my friend had determined that Mark's problem was Bipolar Disorder. My research had actually identified the problem, but now there was a professional diagnosis to support my suspicions and fears.

The therapist took Mark off of the Ritalin immediately! Mark had gone for months taking various Selective Serotonin Re-uptake Inhibitors (SSRIs) ending with Ritalin (not an SSRI)—*none of which were formulated for treating Bipolar Disorder.*

Mark's doctor dug back through her case files and noted that her original inclination had been to diagnose him as bipolar, but, absent a supporting family history of mental illness, she had settled on ADHD and depression as the real problem. Now, given all that had happened, she prescribed Lamictal and sent us home again.

Four days later, Mark walked into the kitchen, put his arms lovingly around me, and said, "I love you so much. It feels like I have been out of my body for so long."

In the weeks that followed, as we inquired into the medical (and mental) background of various family members, we uncovered a long history of mental illness, suicides, and odd stories about relatives who were labeled eccentric or just lazy. As Mark slowly, painfully, began talking about his childhood and I began asking questions of his family, huge gaps of time about which he had no knowledge or memories were filled by stories from his dad and siblings.

Slowly, a picture began to emerge from the recesses of Mark's mind, and the months between his accurate diagnosis and our writing this book have been a journey of constant change and adjustment as we struggle at times to learn to live with this illness.

We were compelled to write this book because, for Mark, there was a ton of information about and support for victims of Bipolar Disorder, some good and some really bad, but for me there was nothing—no support, no guidance, no real help or information.

As a result of my struggles to find out what was wrong, and in a desire to help others avoid the problems I encountered, I finally decided that I needed to pass on to others all I had learned, so I founded the Meehl Foundation and almost immediately created an online presence at www.meehlfoundation.org to help others deal with Bipolar Disorder and to let them know that they are not alone.

Today, with medication and therapy, life is calmer, and after going through what often seemed like the fires of hell, Mark and I are much closer. Today, Mark is on disability and we spend our time identifying triggers and learning new skills. In between learning how to handle everyday strife and stress—skills we once took for granted—Mark now writes and works around the house. Together we research information for the Meehl Foundation and for the seminars and workshops that I have begun to offer.

Our next dream is to create and build a Retreat Center focusing on Bipolar Disorder, a facility that will be run like a Bed and Breakfast and will provide a comfortable, safe, supportive atmosphere in which victims of the illness and their significant others can learn and grow—together.

Bipolar Disorder

"I am married
to the most talented gifted, creative man.
He just happens to be bipolar."
Debra Meehl

The simplest explanation of Bipolar Disorder is that it is a chemical imbalance in the brain. These chemicals affect and control the emotions, and if there is an imbalance, the bipolar person can, and most likely will, be emotionally out of control.

At the present time, the prevailing theory in the medical community is that Bipolar Disorder is genetic, just as are the generally accepted predispositions toward diabetes or heart disease. In addition, and this is equally as important, environmental factors play an important role in this disorder. You must have stressors that push you over the edge. Stressors become the catalysts that cause decompensation. The challenge becomes to live life as fully as possible with it. My example of this is that if you were a Buddhist monk and lived your entire life in the temple, you might not ever experience the intense mood swings that are caused by the stressors of daily living in our society.

This illness affects well over 2.5 million Americans and takes, on average, ten years to diagnose correctly.

Bipolar Disorder affects an increasing number of young people and has the potential to destroy relationships and lives.

There is no cure, no magic pill, and still little knowledge as to its causes and prevention. In over 40 percent of all bipolars there is at least one additional personality disorder at play, usually around issues having to do with addictions and addictive behaviors.

It is clear that along with a pre-existing chemical imbalance in the brain, Bipolar Disorder *must* be prompted by environmental triggers and stresses before it will fully manifest itself.

When discussing environmental triggers it is important to note that we are not referring to environmental triggers such as, say, a person living in a war zone. Sometimes stressors that the rest of us take for granted—one-time or infrequent events like marriage, a job change, an accident, or even childbirth—provide enough stress to set off a bipolar episode.

We have been raised in a society that demands that we strive at any cost to get ahead, to climb the social ladder, to buy that new car and to be successful. Success is clearly defined, and its attainment is demonstrated by an upward-moving lifestyle and standard of living. The constant pressure to conform and to scratch and claw one's way to the top is usually a pressure cooker for the bipolar that begins, all too often, in the achievement-oriented standards that we set for students in high school—and even earlier.

As a result of the environmental stressors and other personality disorders at play, it is quite evident that a combination of drugs and therapy must be employed to treat this disorder effectively and to achieve some sense of "recovery." Without both therapy and medication, your bipolar and you will continue to live on an emotional roller coaster, moving along the track, up and down, down and up, at a high rate of speed—*blindfolded!*

Medication is the foundation, the base, for treating Bipolar Disorder and achieving a state of recovery. Without the correct medication in the body, the bipolar simply lacks the chemical balance necessary to function.

How the medications work, in the simplest terms, is that they help break the neurotransmitter connections that regulate a person's emotions such that every time we see a sunset, for instance, we don't burst into tears—or that we do not rage over the slightest injustice or problem. Without medication, a bipolar will swing through a wide range of emotions and behaviors in an effort to self medicate and escape from the pain. Prescribed medication promotes emotional stability, by balancing the brain's chemicals, thus enabling the bipolar to work intellectually on emotional and other issues.

This is where Cognitive Behavior Therapy comes into play and why it is so important as a supplement to medications. By the time most bipolars are diagnosed (after 10 years, on average), they have developed firmly ingrained patterns in which predictable chemical reactions occur in the brain in response to different situations and triggers. Like a CD, each pattern and reaction is etched into the brain's surface, and thus the emotional trigger is ingrained. So strong is this patterning that it takes both drugs and therapy to achieve results that resemble an optimal state of recovery from this illness. Neither medication alone nor therapy without medication can do the complete job. Medications can establish and maintain a chemical equilibrium, while therapy allows successful changes in behavior to occur. As an example, if your bipolar happens to be a person who usually drives in a road rage, constantly yelling and screaming at other drivers, the medication will help, but your bipolar will still have to change both the thinking about and the ingrained physical reaction to this particular trigger.

Again, there is no blame to be assigned here. The chemicals in the brain have been out of balance for so long, that the bipolar's reaction to situations and triggers has become programmed.

Just as you have learned to respond to situations by programming your mind to react in a specific way, so has the bipolar. The difference for the bipolar is that the intensity of the brain's perception and the often-twisted view of situations and triggers that occur can produce spectacularly inappropriate reactions. Medication will reduce their intensity, but Cognitive Behavior Therapy will be necessary to reprogram the perception of situations and triggers so that reactions become responses. The GOOD news is that it doesn't take ten years of therapy to change ten years of violent reactions and inappropriate behavior. Depending on the skill of the therapist, your bipolar's commitment to change, and your efforts (together with your bipolar) to effect change, it may take only a few months of therapy to produce dramatic changes in both of your lives.

Be absolutely clear: medication and therapy will only go as far as your individual commitments to change will take you.

A commitment to change is like a pebble in a pond; the rippling water affects every inch of the pond's surface. By remaining committed, you can and will see specific, measurable results in time, so do not despair! Yes, there will be challenges and a need to repair your relationship, your family finances and so forth. However, with a commitment to recovery, such repairs can be made and positive change will happen.

For the non-bipolar, this period of recovery is the hardest time! For months—and sometimes years—we certainly knew that there was a problem, but we couldn't find the right help or achieve the proper diagnosis.

As for you, well, you've been living with a Dr. Jekyll and Mr. Hyde character, and it's no wonder you've reached a state of emotional exhaustion!

You never know what emotion to expect from the bipolar. You are tired of walking on eggshells, being criticized while you try to hold the family together, pay the bills, work, fill out all the necessary paperwork, and attend doctors' appointments You're also tired of trying to provide emotional support for your bipolar

What kept us—Deb and Mark—together was (and still is) HOPE, pure and simple. I somehow, instinctively, have always known that the "real" person I love is in there, inside of Mark, because we have both seen glimpses from time to time.

This is why you, too, must change your thinking, so that you're not just waiting for the other shoe drop at any moment. But it takes time to forgive, trust, and live in the present moment.

You must also learn to look at life in six-month and twelve-month intervals. We are often asked, "How is Mark doing? How is his treatment coming? Are you seeing measurable results?" Our answer is generally, "Fine, fine and yes." If you ask these questions at a calm time, when the medications and therapy are cruising along and everything is working, then measurable results are easy to see. If, however, you should ask these questions during a week of raging and depression, then the results are less obvious and the answers less positive.

Bottom line? Some weeks are better than others, and some things seem to have become less significant triggers than in the past. We can see progress, but sometimes life blocks our view. By measuring progress in six- and twelve-month intervals, we can more easily recognize progress. So, when this or that week is hell and you have a manic or depressed person on your hands, look back over the last several months and see if, in the larger sense, there has been progress. If there hasn't, change medications, doctors or therapists and read on.

There are some things that you can do for yourself that will undeniably make a difference in the bipolar's life, and, most importantly, in *your life:*

- ♦ take care of yourself,
- ♦ learn new communication and coping skills to help you and your partner, and
- ♦ find a support group.

We will offer specific information and suggestions about these measures later on.

Depression - what it looks like to the non-bipolar

- Self-absorbed, selfish, demanding, unaware or unconcerned about the needs of others
- Unresponsive, uncommunicative, aloof and/or withdrawn
- Uninterested in sex and dismissive, or distrusting of a partner's tenderness or affection
- Fractious, querulous, combative, contrary, finding fault with everything
- Demeaning and critical of a partner
- Changeable and unpredictable, illogical and unreasonable
- Manipulative
- Pleasant and charming in public and the opposite at home
- Prone to sudden, inexplicable reference to separation or divorce
- Prone to workaholism or avoidance of responsibility
- Increasingly dependent on alcohol and drugs, gambling, spending money
- Obsessively addicted to TV, computer games and computer porn sites, and other compulsive distractions

From *Depression Fallout*, Anne Sheffield, Harper Collins, New York, 2003

Your bipolar's depression doesn't give either of you the right to act like a jackass. We learned this from a therapist who worked with AIDS hospice patients. He used to say to some of them, "You don't have to act like an ass just because you're dying."

Depression does not give anyone the right to behave badly. This is the question that I ask: "If the house were on fire, would you be able to get out of bed or off the couch to get the kids and the dog out?" If the answer is yes, then Mark can get up and do the dishes, take a bath, fix a meal, etc. If the answer is no, he needs to be hospitalized.

Mania - what it looks like to the non-bipolar

♦ Irritable, angry or raging
♦ Racing thoughts, unable to concentrate, unable to hold a thought
♦ Fast talking or talking incessantly
♦ Spending money like a millionaire
♦ Obsessive compulsive
♦ Grandiose ideas such as wanting to start a horse farm even though the bipolar has never owned a horse
♦ Positive thinking (Peter Pan thinking)
♦ Indiscriminate sexual encounters
♦ Wanting sex multiple times a day with a partner
♦ Aggressive, paranoid, psychotic, delusional (last stages)

Mark says that this feels and looks like the "Starship Enterprise" just before it shifts into warp speed. The lights and thoughts start racing toward him and he cannot control his thoughts or focus on any one thought or idea.

Taking
Back
Your
Life

Join a support group

Find a support group in your area. It will provide sanity, an escape, useful tips and a lot of support; thus the name.

There are many support groups for bipolars, but unfortunately, they are often closed to family members. Although we believe this is a terrible decision, we have to accept it. To help, we recommend CODA or Al-Anon as a great place to start looking for a support group for yourself as a non-bipolar living in a bipolar world.

Debra began attending Al-Anon meetings specifically because she could not locate a support group for non-bipolars. Not surprisingly, she found several people in Al-Anon who are also dealing with the same issues, and so the group was able to fill a void until she could start her own *combined* support group for both non-bipolars and bipolars.

She learned three critical slogans in Al-Anon—the three "Cs" . . .

- I did not *cause* this
- I cannot *control* this
- I cannot *cure* this

. . . which leads to the following three valuable conclusions: 1) get off their backs, 2) get out of their way, and 3) get on with your life!

"Detach with love," says Al-Anon.

Detachment is neither kind nor unkind. It does not imply either judgment or condemnation of the person or situation from which we are detaching. It is simply a perspective that allows us to separate ourselves from the adverse effects that another person's illness or addiction can have upon our lives. Detachment helps family members to look at their situations realistically and objectively, thereby making intelligent decisions possible.

In Al-Anon, we learn:[1]

1. *Not to suffer because of the actions or reactions of other people;*
2. *Not to allow ourselves to be used or abused by others in the interest of another's recovery;*
3. *Not to do for others what they can do for themselves;*
4. *Not to manipulate situations so others will eat, go to bed, get up, pay bills, not drink;*
5. *Not to cover up for anyone's mistakes or misdeeds;*
6. *Not to create a crisis; and*
7. *Not to prevent a crisis if it is in the natural course of events.*

All of this became very important once I (Deb) stopped trying to control everything in our lives. Of course, when I did so, the situation followed a natural course of events, some of which were very painful, but as I also learned, most of the time your head does not blow off. It is unpleasant, uncomfortable, and

---

[1] From Al-Anon, "Detach with Love" handout

damn hard, but there is a light at the end of the tunnel. I will say this: if your bipolar is suicidal, you should try to prevent this crisis if at all possible. Not preventing a crisis does not mean forsaking clear boundaries. It also isn't about losing your credit rating or having your house mortgage foreclosed upon because the bills are not paid. That is irresponsible and co-dependent.

There are many support groups for bipolars, but as we have already pointed out, very few for the non-bipolar partner. If, however, you are in a small or remote area or if such support just isn't available, you may have to rely on an on-line support group. The Meehl Foundation provides such an online support group on the Foundation website, which can be found at www.meehlfoundation.org. To join the group, simply follow the links. A search through Yahoo or Google will also provide you with links to many helpful chat groups for bipolars and their partners.

Finally, if you can't find a support group and online support just isn't appealing to you, start a group of your own. The Meehl Foundation provides a course for group facilitators. The website contains useful information on starting and facilitating such a group, and the Foundation staff is always available to provide advice and information by email or telephone.

Boundaries

"No longer am I willing to lose my self-esteem, my self-respect, or my children's well-being, my job, home, possessions, safety, credit, sanity, or my self to preserve a relationship."

Do you remember that quote from Melodie Beatty? We printed it at the very front of this book and repeat it here simply because it is one of the most important understandings that any family member can have about how to become motivated to act, intelligently and purposefully, in the face of Bipolar Disorder.

I am learning how—appropriately and with a sense of high self-esteem—to *choose* to give. I'm learning that I can occasionally decide to give up something during conflict negotiations. However, I am no longer willing to *mindlessly* lose everything I have for the sake of relationships or appearances or in the name of love.

Boundaries are critical to establishing and maintaining a healthy relationship, but I, for one, did not and could not fully understand that until I had memorized that Melodie Beatty quote and used it as an affirmation for months while it was posted on my bathroom mirror. Once I decided that I was totally responsible for my life and my happiness, my relationship and my self-esteem changed. No longer could I shift the responsibility for my life to someone else.

Here are some questions to ask yourself if you think you need to set boundaries.

1. Where do you need boundaries?
   - Are you in financial crisis due to someone else's actions?
   - Is your credit a problem?
2. Do you shift the responsibility for your life to someone else by blaming that person for your current situation?
3. Do you justify some particularly negative or damaging behavior that you would not usually do?
4. By not setting boundaries do you tend to justify your nagging, harping or unreasonableness?

There are few absolutes

Other than the absolutes of the Presence of God and the Power of Love, there are few "*absolutes*"—and *you created them*!

Reflect upon and re-evaluate the "absolutes" in your life. To survive in the bipolar world, you may need to modify or eliminate some of your "absolutes" while reaffirming others. As you do this, involve your bipolar and make a *contract* (verbal at least, perhaps even written) to have fewer of them in your life. The only absolutes I have today are that Mark must take his medication and must not sleep with other women.

Many of us live under the burden of many "absolutes" and in the black-or-white world of the bipolar there are even more. These "musts" and "must nots" can become tremendous triggers as we move through life. In the bipolar world, such self-created absolutes will produce never-ending cascades of emotions that lead to cycling. By reducing the number of absolutes in both of your lives, you will reduce the number of potential triggers, thus significantly reducing the resulting chaos in your lives. So take the time to meditate on the absolutes in your life. See if they really are absolutes instead of just desires, and measure whether they are really that important when compared to all the others. Choose carefully and wisely, but choose only a few.

Set boundaries

Set clear and consistently observed boundaries—defining what you, the non-bipolar, will put up with—particularly with respect to the bipolar's depression or mania. This goes for both adults and children. Once again, Bipolar Disorder is not an excuse for bad behavior.

Explain why the boundaries you set are important. Allow some boundaries to be set for you; there are limits that others in the family believe to be important for you to observe. This doesn't mean that you all should set boundaries on every little thing, all of the time. Take time to contemplate priorities and to settle on those few things that are really important, eliminating or de-emphasizing the rest.

For example, what are the limits on how many days you will you allow your depressed partner to come to bed without taking a shower? Will you move to the couch if this happens? Or will you ask them to sleep in the spare bedroom? How many bounced checks before the debit card is taken back? How many days will you work, pay the bills, take care of the kids and do all the housework while your depressed partner stays in bed? Will you hire help?

Boundaries are important for several reasons, but first and foremost is that they keep you from feeling used, victimized, exhausted or unappreciated.

Every relationship contains itself within boundaries and we all understand that they exist for the benefit of everyone.

If you observe boundaries being violated, immediately find out why—this can be a sign of decompensation—and check the medications. Let the therapist know what happened. Discuss it, figure it out and reset the boundary. Keeping your bipolar child or partner involved in this process obviously increases the chances for long-term success.

Boundaries are designed to protect both the bipolar and yourself from the influences of mania and depression and the racing emotions and behavior that accompany them. Choose carefully and wisely. Work with your partner to communicate your boundaries clearly and to clarify absolutely why they are important.

Will they always work? No! But more often than not they will, and most importantly, boundaries are vital for your own emotional and physical well-being.

Here's a boundary that we believe should be universal, always at the top of the list: *Physical violence against each other and/or children is unacceptable.*

This illness is not an excuse for violence by either party, and abuse of any kind must not be tolerated. The purpose of this book is to help save relationships, not to destroy them, and for us there is nothing more destructive than violence.

If you fear for your physical safety or the safety of your children or pets, call 911. You can explain to the police that your loved one is mentally ill and needs to go to the hospital. It is very important to notify the authorities that they are not usually like this and that their behavior has probably been brought on by medication that is somehow out of balance.

With Bipolar children in particular, it is very important that crystal clear boundaries become part of the normal, everyday life routine. For instance, administering medications is a vitally important boundary, one that can become a supervised daily routine, ensuring that your child is medicated and that this vital routine will become automatic as they prepare for later life on their own.

Finally, clearly define the consequences that will occur for both of you upon any violation of a boundary by either of you. Then discuss and agree upon what resolution or restitution should look like. Remember that consequences must be clear and firm, but the terms of resolution or restitution can change, adjusting to the in-the-moment needs of the relationship. Until an incident brings them into play, they simply represent a plan.

Codependence

Caregiving is: *one person doing for another person what he or she cannot do unassisted in a specific situation*—tasks such as diapering a baby, pushing a wheelchair for the elderly, or gently reminding a person to take medications as prescribed.

Codependence, on the other hand, is: *one person taking responsibility for another person's emotions, behaviors, thoughts, choices or life course while not taking care of his or her self.*

Every time we fall into codependency, consciously or not, we will inevitably begin to feel angry, deeply resentful, unappreciated, maliciously victimized, and most assuredly "used."

Like so much of life, this is all about balance. One of the hardest lessons for the non-bipolar to learn is to distinguish the fine art of balance when deciding what needs to be done for the bipolar— and what does not. Most non-bipolars are natural-born caregivers (which is not a bad thing), but sometimes this driving motivation causes you, the caregiver, to lose your emotional balance. When this happens, you will invariably find yourself with an emotional and addicted cripple on your hands, and you will rapidly become an emotional wreck.

Non-bipolars can be driven to attempt to "fix" and control everything in an effort to regain "normalcy," often at the cost of health and emotional happiness.

So how do you know which behavior is helpful and which is simply codependent? Start with your feelings, then *become the "observer" of what's going on.*

For example, if your bipolar cannot remember to take medication, try to empower him or her by *asking,* "Do you have any idea about how to get that done?" If you don't get an answer, make suggestions—like writing with dry-erase marker on the mirror, using flip-top medication boxes, or other more off-the-wall ideas. If your bipolar is just being stubborn and doesn't want to take the meds, you will soon become aware of that. By becoming the observer rather than the victimized participant you will be able to make good decisions based on the information at hand.

Some bipolars need only a reminder because they often have short-term memory loss, which is a predictable side effect of medications and the illness. They really do need help. And this is one of the magic keys to managing the situation.

Nagging, needling or harping is co-dependent behavior. It may actually serve to reinforce the very behavior you do not want.

The two things that changed my life the fastest were going to Al-Anon meetings, and reading Melodie Beatty's wonderful book, *"The Codependents' Guide to the Twelve Steps."*

In our case, Mark is not an alcoholic, but he comes from a long line of alcoholics, and some of the behaviors he displays were almost certainly learned from the alcoholics in his early life. I first went to Al-Anon for the same reason everyone does, *to fix him*. I stayed because *it fixed me*. I learned to take care of my own emotions and that my life was my own. I learned to choose to stop living unconsciously. That knowledge turned out to be one of the biggest gifts I could ever have given to Mark.

Again, communication is the key. I try not to assume anything, and I try to remember that I am a partner. I also constantly bear in mind that as easy as it is for the bipolar to become addicted, it is just as easy for the non-bipolar to be codependent, which leads us to become unreasonable, irritable and nagging.

In *"The Codependents' Guide to the Twelve Steps,"* the first step is: ***"We admitted to ourselves that we were powerless over others—that our lives had become unmanageable."***

The truth is, we *are* powerless over both Bipolar Disorder and the person who has this disorder. We can state our feelings, beliefs and concerns, but we have no control over another's behavior.

Do I leave or do I stay?

This is the 64 thousand dollar question, isn't it?

As Iyanla Vanzant notes in one of her books, "When people show you who they are, believe them."

I had help from my therapist with this decision. Our first therapist was a no-holds-barred kind of guy. I asked two questions: What is the best-case scenario for Mark, and what is the worst-case scenario? He told me that the best case would be that the chemical imbalance would be brought under control with medication and then, with behavior therapy, Mark would begin to under-stand his triggers and life would become better, maybe even "good."

The therapist, though, cautioned me that he believed that Mark would never again be able to live in a fast-paced, work-driven career (or even home) environment. He did believe, he said, that—given Mark's near-genius IQ—he would find something that would eventually bring in an income but that Mark would probably never again function effectively in the traditional workplace.

The worst-case scenario would be that Mark would not take his medication and would therefore make no attempt at therapy and as a result would kill himself to stop the pain inside—or he might kill me by accident, such as in a road rage incident.

At that moment, I burst into tears, followed by sobs and total body heaving. It took about 20 minutes for me to recover. I did not know it at the time, but he had told Mark the same thing the day before followed by a description of what it was like living in a mental institution. This may not be the proper therapy for everyone, but it was perfect for Mark. The therapist had captured his complete attention—and Mark wasn't even fully medicated yet! He also told Mark to plan on about five years of weekly therapy—there were a lot of issues to deal with, he emphasized—but it could perhaps take as little as two years.

To Mark's credit, he made an absolute commitment to the therapist, in writing, to work toward recovery, whatever it might take.

Actions always speak louder than words, and to this day Mark is still 100% committed to do whatever it takes to recover and function.

For me the issue had to do with both his level of commitment to his own recovery *and* to our relationship. You see, he decided he loved our life together more than he hated taking medication or doing therapy.

Taking care of yourself

One of the first things that happens when a diagnosis of Bipolar Disorder is confirmed is that ***your needs***—physical, emotional, spiritual and every other kind—get put on hold for a while.

It is exactly the same as if your partner had cancer. Everything suddenly seems to revolve around the sick person, particularly once the diagnosis is made and medications and therapy begin. This scenario isn't bad, it's just the way it is. But you need to begin taking care of yourself as soon as you can.

Schedule an appointment with your family doctor and transmit accurately the bipolar's medical history and the facts about all that is happening in your house. Let him know that you are dealing with a family member who is bipolar and reveal what that looks like for you on a daily basis.

Get a complete physical examination, including comprehensive blood work. Discuss depression (yours) and how the doctor will want to treat it if it should become an issue for you. This will also allow your physician to watch your tests for signs of depression-related changes within you. Well-documented statistics show that approximately 80% of all non-bipolar partners will suffer from some level of depression and will need medication for depression as well as personal therapy.

Once you have been under a certain amount of stress for a long period of time, your own serotonin levels are likely to become depleted, which could lead you to depression. Fortunately, medication can replenish your serotonin levels, and you will again be fine.

One more time, there is no blame involved here. Any depression you might suffer is a natural consequence of stress in your life. In this case, of course, it is a huge occurrence. So do not forget your own medical needs. If anyone needs to stay healthy, it is you.

Meet with the therapist occasionally, not only to check on progress for your bipolar, but also to check on yourself. Living with a bipolar is difficult business, and the constant changes manifested by your bipolar make it hard on everyone. As rewarding as a loving and caring relationship can be, it isn't easy living in the bipolar world.

If for any reason you think or suspect that your partner has been intimate with someone else, you will also need to have tests run for HIV, hepatitis and any other possible STDs. This is one more aspect of personal wellness and self-care. After all, it is better to endure the tests and enjoy peace of mind than to have any surprises or problems crop up later.

A woman I know, we will call her Jane, had to go to her physician and ask to have all the tests run. She said that she had cried for several hours before her appointment but had decided that when she got there she would hold her head high, ask for the tests, get the pelvic exam, and not even flinch. Instead, as soon as the doctor asked why she was there, she burst into tears. She had to explain that her husband had slept with a man in a moment of mania (he later was diagnosed BP), so she was going to need all the tests for sexually transmitted diseases. She said that she was so embarrassed that she wished that the earth would swallow her up that very moment! Her only emotion at the time was intense shame. She then endured HIV testing every six months for a year. Today, though, she is healthy and happy, glad that she had all the tests—she will not have to worry about "what if?"

Taking care of yourself also means scheduling time to be with friends and family and making room for time at the gym, the salon or the spa. Little things like a workout routine, a manicure, a pedicure, a mineral bath or a massage can make a world of difference in how you feel, and it needn't be expensive. For instance, you can get a great massage at any massage school, and with a little imagination you can create your own little spa in your bathroom at home. Take control. Let people know what nurturing gifts you will accept in the future. I treasure a massage gift over all others. If I am too busy or just too tired to leave the house, I'll fill up the bath tub, light some candles (even in the daytime), put on the music, grab an affirmations book and a glass of wine, and soak for as long as it takes to relax and to feel whole again. The fact is, on most days I can have everything set up and ready in ten minutes, spend 20 minutes in the tub, and in 30 minutes be a totally new woman—or, at least, feel like one!

One of the biggest dangers in taking care of your bipolar is that you can become so wrapped up in that process that you forget to take care of yourself.

Bottom line, if you get sick, who is going to take care of your bipolar and you? Yes, take your vitamins, exercise, see a doctor if you need to. When you are healthy you will find that your relationships are healthier, too.

Connect with God, Spirit, Allah...

Let me say here that in our family we use the word 'God' loosely. So if you would rather call it the Power of the Universe, Mother Earth, Higher Power, Infinite Spirit, Buddha, Allah, or something else, that is fine with us. Please do not get hung up on the words. It is the connection and energy that is most important to us. As we continue here, though, we will use the word God—it is shorter and is what we grew up with as children.

All religions clearly state that through a relationship with God you will find peace, hope, balance and healing. You need someone who is always on your side, and for that, God is not a bad choice.

Living in the bipolar world, your emotional and spiritual health can take a beating. Therapy helps and is a critically important component of personal well-being, but it cannot provide immediate comfort and solitude. For this you need a perception of God, a technique for meditation, and an awareness of the healing energy that comes from those places.

We learned early on that mental, spiritual and emotional well-being are truly connected. If you eliminate any one of those facets from your life, or if you neglect even one, the others will come crashing down, too, and will stop serving you. However, it is not as delicate a balance for a non-bipolar family member as it is for the bipolar.

For the non-bipolar, well-being can be equated with walking on a ledge carved into the side of a precipitous cliff. The ledge may be quite wide at times, wide enough so you can swing from one side to the other, compensating for changes as you go. For the bipolar, on the other hand, the ledge is always as narrow as a tightrope.

For both of the people in such a relationship, however, the notion of God is critical. If you are the non-bipolar, the God concept grounds you in the midst of your bipolar's mania and depression and reaffirms that you really are not alone, thus widening your ledge. For the bipolar, God is the balancing bar that enables him or her to traverse the tightrope. A relationship with God will tend to foster balance and support.

We believe that *Mindfulness* leads toward emotional and spiritual well-being through the development and use of mantras and prayers that can help to break or shorten the manic and depressive stages. Through the diligent application of *Mindfulness*, both you and your bipolar can become more acutely aware of your individual emotional states, alert to triggers, fully conscious of shifts in feelings, and in control of reactions to the environment around you.

We use a mantra or prayer to refocus our minds away from the cycle of thought running in the bipolar's mind, thus enabling the bipolar to stop racing thoughts and negative ideas that we call "playing in the sandbox." The sooner the bipolar can stop playing in that imaginary place the fewer negative effects mania and depression will have on the members of the household.

It has been our experience that the well-known 23rd Psalm from the Old Testament is a very effective tool for breaking through mania. Once again, you need someone who is always on your side—and God is waiting to help.

Develop your own support system

As the partner, son or daughter of a bipolar, surround yourself with supportive friends and family. Frequently, you will need someone to talk to, a person who understands what you are going through and who will be a source of strength. A support group or a club will give you access to many such friends, people who will have coffee with you or simply talk with you on the phone, folks who will understand, care and be supportive.

It is all too easy to allow yourself to become isolated, which can be very damaging to your own mental health. You need to interact with non-bipolars, and you need time away from the house, time to focus on yourself and your needs. You need to have someone who will just listen to you. If you have no one close by, easily reachable resources of this kind, find a chat room on the Internet that operates for friends and family of bipolars. One is on the Meehl Foundation's website, which is located at www.meehlfoundation.org. It focuses on helping bipolars and their families to live in the bipolar world.

Practical
Financial
Matters

Protect your credit

Now, if you are a multi-millionaire this may not apply to you. But if you're not independently wealthy and the bipolar in your life has previously made reckless financial decisions and/or has gone on spending sprees caused by mania . . . *MAKE SURE THAT THE BIPOLAR IN YOUR LIFE IS NOT AN AUTHORIZED SIGNER ON ANY OF YOUR ACCOUNTS*—credit cards, checking, savings, etc. You should have **one** joint account, or one that the bipolar can access and use. Even bipolars need money and a small, shared account is the best option. The shared account allows the bipolar to grocery shop, run errands and be a participant in the daily running of the house.

We are reminded of the story of a gentleman who went out in a manic moment and purchased 13 pink Cadillacs. It is not uncommon for couples to find themselves thousands of dollars in debt as a result of uncontrolled spending during a manic episode. This is not good.

By limiting the access to any spending account (credit cards, checking, savings), you limit the occurrences and the impacts of uncontrolled spending, and you thereby protect your family's credit. This often means that the non-bipolar is the partner who will be responsible for all financial decisions affecting the family. Although you can, and should involve the bipolar in some of the decisions, or at least a discussion of expenses, the final decision should be yours.

This will mean that any credit cards your bipolar has should be in *his or her name only* with small credit limits ($500 or less) so as to limit the impact of uncontrolled spending.

Your name must not appear on any of your bipolar's credit cards or credit applications. This will help insure that you and your family retain the ability to use your own credit cards when necessary and that you will have the credit necessary to purchase a house, a car, a trip, etc. This also means that you may need to *consider* your joint ownership in your house, car, boat, etc.

When we bought the home that we live in, Mark signed a quitclaim deed to the house so that title would be registered in my name only. This protects our home from a lien being placed on it, as well as from anything that may happen to Mark, whether medical or criminal. The same thing holds true for your car and insurance. If your partner should be in an accident involving drinking or drugs and if a lawsuit follows from that, you can be assured that if you haven't protected those assets, your home and other possessions would be the first to be seized. Check with an attorney in your state and know your rights and responsibilities.

We often hear of the remorse that bipolars invariably express over the results of their uncontrolled spending. Spouses will point out that new medications are being used, or that their partner is remorseful and apologetic and has promised to never go on a shopping spree again. This is wonderful, and we are always happy to hear such remorse and promises. However, what happens the next time your bipolar's medication doesn't work or needs changing? And *there will be a next time* (thus the term *cycling*)! Unless you have arranged to limit access to your accounts, they will spend, spend, spend—and you will be responsible.

Uncontrolled spending can take many forms. The need to shop and spend is at times consuming for a bipolar, and is not necessarily limited to big-ticket items.

As an example, there is simply nothing more dangerous for us than to let Mark loose in a grocery store with a credit card. He will purchase additional food for guests, snacks, treats for the dog, and items to celebrate the change in the phase of the moon. During a manic phase, a simple trip to the store for milk will likely result in a $60.00 shopping spree. Is this uncontrolled spending? Not according to Mark, who rationalizes, " . . . of course, every house needs a couple of cans of Anchovies and pickled elephant toes in its pantry!"

If you are currently in financial trouble or think you may be getting into trouble, do not just bury your head in the sand; seek professional help. Do not wait until the creditors are knocking on the door. Waiting will only make the crisis worse. Seek a credit counselor or debt consolidator—there are many listed on the web or in the phone directory—and interview them. You do not have to go with the first one who is presented to you. If you think that you may lose your home, seek a Bankruptcy Attorney immediately. Being proactive here is the key; waiting until the last minute limits your choices. Please protect yourself.

File for disability as soon as possible

The bottom line is that many bipolars are unable to work or can barely keep working for very long, thus they put a tremendous stress on any relationship and its financial position.

One of the most common reasons bipolar families give for not filing for disability is that they believe the condition to be temporary and that the bipolar will get better and/or be able to return to work soon.

Underlying all that, though, is the probability that the family perceives disability as a weakness and that there is a stigma attached to "disability" that is at times demeaning.

We, on the other hand, tend to look at disability as *an opportunity to contribute to your family's financial health at a time when you truly need it.* You receive a check *because you have earned it and qualify for a certain amount.* Besides, there is nothing that says you can't stop the process at any time, such as when it's possible to continue working. However, disability filing is a long process that can take up to a year and sometimes longer, and it involves many people.

The sooner you file, the sooner you will receive a check. The process for Mark took 13 months, and we were fortunate not to have been denied the first time, *which is very common.* There is a 6-month waiting period, during which you must be completely unemployed. For Mark, there were six long months of unemployment followed by an incident in which SSI lost his paper work, forcing us to collect all the information from the doctors again. Next, his caseworker quit, and then his paper work was transferred to another caseworker who already had a complete caseload.

To file for disability, go to your nearest Social Security office. You can find the address in the Government pages of your phone book.

We recommend that the non-bipolar spouse/partner or family member handle the entire disability filing process. If ever there was a process designed to trigger a bipolar-like rage (even for a non-bipolar person), this is it! It's even worse for the bipolar.

You will also want to get a letter supporting the disability claim from your physicians and therapist. When talking to anyone from Social Security *you must get his or her name and phone extension*. Keep a phone log with the date, time, and a summary of what the call was about, along with any promises made by the person to whom you speak.

By the way, there are companies that will file the claim for you, for a fee. You can locate them on the Internet. One example is ALSUP, INC., a firm that charges $750 for their services. Their information is in the Resource Guide. If, for any reason, you are denied, you pay nothing. Many of these companies produce a high rate of success the first time around. Had I known about them in the beginning I would have used them. Between the doctor appointments, VA appointments (Mark served in the military), medication checks, therapy, and all the other stressors in our lives at the time, I would gladly have paid for their services.

Very importantly, *copy all the paperwork that you send in, and send it by certified mail and request a return receipt.*

No one has ever said that the disability process is easy or pleasant—or free of obstacles. You should be aware that it is not uncommon to be turned down on your first application.

If that should happen, do not despair! Immediately file an appeal and then *re-file a claim for disability.* You will, in essence, have two claims going at the same time, and the winner will be the one that approves you first.

Another option is to enlist the help of your U.S. Congressman. Call your representative's office and speak with the "liaison for mental health issues." That person may be able to get the process moving and cut through a great deal of red tape. Don't feel as though you are imposing in any way. Such representation is one of the services you pay for when you pay your taxes.

Yet another choice is to call your state's Bar Association and ask for a list of attorneys who deal with Social Security claims. I have spoken to a number of people who have used an attorney after being initially denied, and not one of them was denied a second time.

Through all of this, keep in mind that the people at Social Security are overworked and understaffed, so getting specific dates and reasonable timelines is important.

As an example, if at the end of four weeks you haven't received a notice that you were looking for, call them and chase down your answer. They may have forgotten, possibly lost something—*who knows?* But if you don't stay on top of the situation, nothing will get done! Again, this is why it is so important that a non-bipolar handle such frustrating and potentially "triggering" situations.

When Mark's caseworker quit and his file somehow got buried, he went nuclear and threatened to decapitate an unsuspecting substitute caseworker. As helpful as this threat may have seemed to Mark, it was easier to get his file moving again by being polite and persistent. One result of that change of strategy was that we were able to bring the new caseworker into total agreement that Mark should get disability.

In any event, file as soon as possible. Keep a positive attitude and expectations. And *file for Interim Benefits while your claim is being processed*.

Yes, **Interim Benefits**. If you qualify because of your economic status, you can receive a partial payment as the primary disability claim process goes forward. Ask about the possibilities, and apply if you qualify. Your caseworker will help you with the entire process.

VA benefits

One of the more brilliant things Mark ever did was to join the Army. The experience itself left a fair amount of scarring, but the ultimate result turned out to be that he qualifies for Veteran's Benefits.

If your bipolar is a veteran, contact your local VA field office and discover what services they offer for treating Bipolar Disorder and have them inform you about the intake process for your area.

The VA observes a number of protocols for the treatment of Bipolar Disorder, but their rules and procedures generally focus on "helping" rather than on "treating." You will need to know what medication options exist, what the side effects of each drug might be, procedures for changing medication, and limitations regarding the conditions under which such changes can occur. Be sure to ask, "What is the in-patient treatment program?" and "How is admission handled?"

Knowledge is power and is definitely respected in this environment.

The advantage to VA treatment is the cost. Bipolar Disorder is an expensive illness to treat, and Welfare benefits will only go so far. So it behooves you to take full advantage of your Veterans benefits as available.

For the record, although you may be using the VA for your medications and are participating in their program, you still may—and occasionally should—seek the advice of outside professionals.

If you are applying for VA Disability as a result of your time in service, contact your local VFW office or American Legion post. Each of these organizations can provide you with an advocate who will help you through the application process.

The biggest oversight that people commit when applying for disability is not to use an experienced advocate for all communications with the VA. Let your advocate work for you and guide you through the process.

In preparing for this process, get a copy of your military medical file and notify your doctor and therapist that you will need letters from them. There is a particular format for these letters, and your advocate will be able to furnish you with a copy of the format, which you can then pass on to your practitioners.

Finally, be prepared for a wait. The filing process for either VA benefits or State Disability takes time (at least several months) to be approved. As with filing for Social Security Disability, the longer you wait, the longer you will have to wait (delay seems to feed upon itself). Get on this now!

Buy term insurance

It is almost impossible to get life insurance if you are mentally ill. Sure, they'll insure the non-bipolar, but they will not cover the sufferer. As unfair as it seems, that is how the system works. This restriction certainly doesn't help with insuring that there will be money for the family in the event that something should happen.

Fortunately, there is term insurance. This low cost form of policy often does not require a physical examination or a check of medical history, so it may be a great way to insure your bipolar and the future.

In addition, premiums are much lower than ordinary life insurance, which means that you can actually purchase a larger policy for the same amount of money as you could normally get with a more traditional "whole life" or "universal life" policy.

It is very important to recognize that these "term" policies will not pay benefits if death should occur by suicide within a certain period of time (usually within two years of the purchase of the policy). However, since suicide should never be an option for a bipolar, this clause will give you a finite period of time in which you can deal with any suicide issues by reminding the bipolar that suicide would void the policy and take away the monetary benefits that it promises.

Set up trust accounts

As the non-bipolar parent of children, make sure that your will specifies that if you should precede your bipolar partner in death, the estate will immediately be set up in trust accounts. These accounts can generate a monthly income for a partner, be set aside for future lump sum payments, or otherwise established to protect everyone.

The purpose of the trust system is to avoid giving a large amount of money to a manic spouse or child and having it disappear. By funding a trust account that earns a fair interest rate, you can protect your bipolar partner and provide a monthly income to support them and any children. This income can make all the difference in the world.

Find the right job

For the bipolar, the workaday world can present an invitation to disaster. Dramatic mood changes and frequent mood cycling make it very difficult—and sometimes virtually impossible—for a bipolar to work at a regular job, to be consistent in workplace behavior, to maintain regular attendance and level of performance, or to maintain a good working relationship with others.

For you, the caregiver, family member or friend, it can be equally difficult to care for or about a bipolar and to adjust your schedule and needs to match or complement theirs.

Obviously, the financial stress caused from intermittent work or chronic unemployment can also be a major source of problems for any couple and even more so for the family.

Since most bipolars and their partners are highly intelligent and creative individuals, it makes sense to seek out career paths for them that will utilize these strengths. If possible, find work that is personally fulfilling and allow the bipolar to do what he or she loves to do as well as you the caregiver.

Most Community Colleges have Assessment Tests that will help find different careers/jobs that will fit the needs, both professional and personal, of the bipolar individual.

As a suggestion, consider jobs that provide significant degree of scheduling flexibility, such as sales, consulting, construction, art, etc.

And here's a radical idea—if the bipolar can't find appropriate and satisfying work, then the challenge becomes . . . create it!

Here is our personal story . . .

"The first thing I (Debra) did was to *create the possibility of having the **perfect** job.* I started by having a friend coach me in believing in the possibility that somewhere there was "the perfect job" for me, and that was the heading I wrote on my first journal page: THE POSSIBILITIES.

My belief system at the time held little in the way of possibilities because all of the negative messages I had received during my life until that time had convinced me that:

- it just does not happen to the average person, and
- some people just get lucky, but I am not one of them.

One of my major criteria was to find a job in which I would have a flexible work schedule (because of Mark's illness).

As I continued to set my sights on a new job I soon found out that I wanted more, much more. The list grew quickly, from work schedule flexibility to:

- travel time,
- acknowledgement for talents,
- fulfillment,
- benefits like medical insurance and dental insurance
- a 401k retirement plan,
- paid time-off.

Of course, there were also basic issues like how much I would be paid, one determination of which would be based on my personal definition that prosperity is: . . . "the *ability to have, do or be what you want, when you want and with whom you want.*"

I also knew that I had to be touched, moved and inspired by my work; it needed to reflect my true passion and allow me to demonstrate what I was really good at.

The date on that first journal page was 10/23/03 . . . and in June of 2004 we started the Meehl Foundation.

You see, all I needed was to become absolutely clear about what I wanted, to release my limiting beliefs, and to get out of the way and let God deliver it. To this day I am truly in awe of all that has fallen into place for this to happen.

We have also found that many bipolars are self-employed or work for small companies, environments in which they either run the show or have considerable control over their work environment, time schedule, and so forth.

Small companies, in our experience, also tend to be a good deal more understanding of the bipolar's needs. Therefore, it is often possible to arrange to allow the bipolar to work alone and to control the amount of stress present at any given time, or to surround themselves with a supportive group of co-workers.

Because the structures are less flexible and the expectations more highly codified, the impersonal world of the large corporation can be a disaster for many bipolars and should be carefully evaluated before a bipolar decides to work in one.

History bears out that most bipolars who find success in the work world are entrepreneurs. They often don't make good employees, but they do make great leaders. Some of the most gifted, intelligent and talented people in business today are bipolar.

Nonetheless, we recommend giving up the promise of riches for the promise of stability and calm.

The other idea to remember is that there are many definitions for work. A hobby can turn into a very profitable little business and become work, just as writing this book has become Mark's work.

Our advice is to find work that is both financially rewarding and personally fulfilling. If you are the bipolar who has to bear the burden of being the primary wage earner and the person who must endure the pressures of daily life *plus* those uniquely present in the bipolar world, the only workable solution is to truly enjoy the work you do. *If you don't enjoy what you are doing, change jobs.* Being at a job that you hate eight hours a day on every working day creates more stress and triggers than it's worth, and from a health standpoint alone it will be better for you to change jobs just as soon as you realize what's happening to you.

Find your life purpose

"The future belongs to those who believe in the beauty of their dreams."
Eleanor Roosevelt.

Your life purpose will always be bigger than you or your job. It will be a way to serve God, humanity and the planet. And it will touch, move and inspire you.

Here are some big questions to ask yourself:

◆ What is God's vision of me?
◆ What does that look like and feel like?
◆ What do I need to release?
◆ Is there anything else I need to know?

Once you find your purpose and begin to live it, the comfort, joy, prosperity, and peace in your life will just seem to fall into place.

Most bipolars are highly creative and intelligent people who tend to think "outside the box" and effectively tap hidden talents and skills, which means that as a caregiver, family member or friend of a bipolar you should let go of any preconceived ideas you might have about the restrictions and limitations under which you believe the bipolar may be operating.

Bipolars, in general, tend to be people who are not happy working for the local hamburger place. They seem to have a sense of something bigger, a void within themselves that needs to be fulfilled. For example, Benjamin Franklin had 32 jobs, eight wives and 17 children. I think you get the point here.

There will be a moment when peace washes over you, or you instinctively know the answer to a question that you have asked. Don't be alarmed when this happens, it's supposed to.

When pointed in the right direction, toward their gifts and talents, bipolars seem to prosper both emotionally, spiritually and financially.

Our
Core
Beliefs

The story
we tell ourselves

Do you know the difference between a story and reality? Reality must take up time and space. The mathematical formula for this is: Time x Space = Reality. Stated another way: Reality is what happens in time and space.

Our life stories are always colored by our learned cultural heritage, felt experiences and related perceptions. Another way to say this is that we calculate reality in the past by our impressions of what happened, not necessarily by the literal time-space event that occurred.

That is why when 50 people witness a crime there are 50 different stories about what happened.

Picture this: I stand up with a gun and shoot someone. At the moment this happens it is reality, but five minutes after the event it is a story, and for each person who tells it the story is different. Their uniquely individual emotions, perceptions and reasoning faculties have taken over.

Does this mean that "bad things" don't happen to people? No, you can bet they do! But it is the constant retelling of *our* story in *our* minds that keeps us stuck, living the same event (*or interpretation of the event*) over and over again. "Stuff" happens to us all the time; it is what we do with those experiences, how we process them, that shapes our lives and makes the difference.

Our life stories are all punctuated with good times and bad times, pleasant events and unpleasant events. But some of us focus most of the time on the positive stuff, while others of us focus on and talk about the bad stuff.

For example, my grandmother used to tell about all of the "bad" things that happened to her: how she walked five miles in a snow blizzard to go to school; how in her family there was only stale bread to eat; how she lived through the depression; and how my mother died when I was two years old. The list went on and on, and it was all about how *bad* her life was. She almost never focused on the positive.

I believe that it was probably all those years of negative thinking and talking that led, finally, to the physical and mental illnesses that ruled and *controlled* her life until she died. She stopped living in the present and never looked for the positive in her life. Trust me when I tell you that this has an effect on children.

Do you recall the groundbreaking research that was done with Pavlov's Dog? Remember that after the experimenter had conditioned the animal repetitively by providing food every time he rang the bell, he would just ring the bell and the dog would salivate. Think of this as you talk to someone about a "bad event" that has happened to him or her. Observe how that person describes the event and responds emotionally. The vocabulary of the description and the emotionality of the response will provide a great deal of insight into the history and the upbringing of that person. If you observe closely, listen hard and ask good questions you can begin to understand why the storyteller chose to respond in that specific way.

Most of our storytelling (some call it "self-talk") conjures up lots of emotions. In fact, that's one of the reasons we tell stories--we like the *feel* of it. You see, a re-telling of the emotion-based story inevitably produces the same feelings and/or emotions as did the event itself.

Now ask yourself, "What negative stories do I keep telling myself?"

Here are just a few for you to practice on: "Life is hard." "There is no one who understands." "You must scratch and claw your way to the top." "You can't trust anyone."

What do *you* get out of stories like these? Is it a "somebody's done somebody wrong song" that plays over and over in your mind?

In your unique position, right now, you may say, "Well, you just don't understand, he/she lied to me, left me for another, slept with someone else,

stole all my money, ruined my credit"—
the list goes on and on.

Ask yourself these questions:

1. Does my story allow me to be a victim?
2. Does it permit me to justify a behavior I wouldn't otherwise allow myself?
3. Does it let me put off things I consider unpleasant?
4. Does it tempt me to shift the responsibility for my life to someone else?

Now consider this information in regards to the bipolar in *your* life and remember that the real issue revolves around an emotional disorder.

If your bipolar is in a state of depression, it's likely that his or her perceptions are grossly inaccurate, because the symptoms of depression and mania are patently illogical, completely unreasonable, unfailingly contrary, and filled with fault-finding about everything from work to relationships to money to the kids—and most likely even to the dog and the neighbor down the street!

Everything is colored by the depression and/or mania that is part and parcel of Bipolar Disorder.

And don't forget, the "story" has been colored by the illness for years and years (usually for at least ten years prior to accurate diagnosis).

Armed with this knowledge you can perhaps understand and develop some compassion for the effort it takes for a bipolar to achieve stability. Bipolars don't just have one or two life traumas, or tragedies, they have at least ten years' worth.

Practice mindfulness

Mindfulness is the ability to watch your thoughts just go on by.

My practice of conscious mindfulness allows me to stay calm and centered at all times—even when Mark is in the midst of an episode—so that I can help *him* stay grounded.

In my mind's eye I see this as like holding a fishing pole with a fish flopping about on the end of the line, out of your control. I don't run up and down the stream to reel my fish in, I stand still and then slowly start reeling it in. If I stay centered, Mark can flop around in chaos but I do not have to respond or react to his chaos. I can be watchful, mindful and centered, at the same time helping to move him toward centeredness, as well, by applying the techniques we will discuss later.

Again, we all have stories that we tell ourselves, and most of the time we are unconscious about how they are affecting our thinking and our actions. Often we tend to judge others, to criticize their behaviors, and to attribute some arbitrary meaning to everything that comes our way (based on our life experience). Mindfulness returns to us the power of our own minds by enabling us simply to passively "watch our thoughts" and the reactions of our bodies to these thoughts, then to make objective, conscious choices as to what we are thinking in any moment, how we are judging any person, and what "stories" we choose to invent about any event. As we master this skill we find ourselves able to block out any unwanted thoughts.

Mark offers a wonderful example of mindfulness by likening his thought patterns to wind blowing through the trees. As he watches the wind move through the leaves of the trees in the park near our home, he doesn't label the trees, nor does he evaluate the motion or power of the wind; he just *experiences* the wind. So it is, he says, with his thoughts; he doesn't label them or evaluate them, he just lets them blow through his mind and *experiences* them.

An opposite example, one of *not* being mindful, might be a time when, after having driven your car for some time, you arrive at your destination and simply cannot remember anything about "getting there"—you have completely "zoned out." Or have you stood by your sink washing dishes, then suddenly realizing that the dishes are done but all you can remember is that you've been thinking about the bills you have to pay? You have no idea what you did to get the dishes cleaned and dried!

Most of us do this sort of thing all the time. We become unconscious to our thinking and then wonder, for instance, why we missed something someone has said to us.

Next time you have the opportunity to be with a small child, notice that children generally never miss the little things. As you walk through a park, the child will see a small bug on the sidewalk or a beautiful flower beside the trail. Children have not been conditioned *not* to be in the present moment—yet—so they are fully able to experience every detail in a moment.

The first step in achieving mindfulness is to sit still, as Mark does, and watch your thoughts go by as though they were items on a conveyor belt. One passes, then the next, then the next . . . no judging, critiquing or attaching any significance to your thoughts, just observe them passing through your mind.

It will take some practice, but once you learn how to do this you will become aware of how much your "stories" run your life.

Actually (we think you'll agree), it's no wonder that so many people are so unhappy. If your mind is negative, or if it's constantly telling you a negative story, how can you project positive thoughts and live positively?

There is no doubt in my mind, the most useful tool that I have in my toolbox is **_Mindfulness_**. Everything else falls into place when I implement this in my life, and you have that opportunity, too.

What are the final results of this exercise? For me, the story is this:

- I am no longer the victim.
- I have control of what I am thinking, and that makes the biggest difference in my marriage, too.
- I am more able to deal with just the facts of the situation.
- I do not need to tell the story of how much wrong someone has done me, so I can easily move on. (*Note: This is very important when living in the bipolar world. It enables me to not take anything personally when I am confronted with Mark's mania or depression; I can also reduce or eliminate many of the negative stories that I may have built into my life.*) I might add that this is also one of the hardest concepts to learn and takes a lot of practice; I'm sure we all get lots of mileage and attention out of a really good "story."

The way in which mindfulness helps Mark is that it enables him to recognize and talk about the triggers that produce episodes, thus helping us to learn why they set him off. By being mindful, we both are better able deal with, and avoid, potential triggers. Of course, this requires conscious communication by both of us and a commitment to honesty and openness in discussing triggers. Mindfulness helps here, too. Because we are both better able to communicate *exactly what is going on* for each of us, I know that I get a clearer picture of how the triggers are affecting both Mark and me. He agrees.

The other element of mindfulness— not to be overlooked—is being aware of, and careful about, what we put into our minds. Listening to the radio play another "somebody done somebody wrong song" is not the way to lift one's self out of depression. Neither is watching a sad movie. Some of the best research done on healing has shown that positive input produces positive output. Watching and listening to humor and comedy, for example, produces happier interactions between the people who are receiving these "happy" inputs. On the "good days," our house is filled with laughter and humor. On the "bad days," good humor eases the pain.

Learn to meditate

Meditation can be defined as the ability to quiet the mind and create a space between thought.

Again, this takes a lot of practice. I know there many Christians (just as one example) who are uncomfortable about or unfamiliar with meditation. They shouldn't be, of course. After all, Jesus went into the desert for 40 days to quiet his own mind and center himself, to gather the strength and courage to know that his life was on the right track. No doubt about it, Jesus was meditating. And, remembering that prayer is a form of meditation, here are three scriptural passages we recommend reading:

Psalm 46:10: *"Be still and know that I am God,"*

2Corinthians 10:5: *"Take every thought captive to Christ"*

Romans 12:2: *"Be transformed by the renewing of your mind, then you will know what God's will is."*

When we can release the ego and go into that quiet place inside the mind, we can be changed.

There are many ways to meditate, and there is no "right way." There is only the way that works for you.

There is focused breathing, where you think of just your breath going in and out of your lungs. You can even add a counting system—*in* one, *out* two, *in* three, *out* four—that helps to still the mind, and trains it to be focused.

There is focusing on your breath going in your right nostril and going out though your left nostril. Don't block either nostril with a finger, just "see" the breath going in one and coming out the other—you may be surprised at how quickly you get the hang of this.

I teach this technique in our support groups, and most of the bipolars say they use it to effectively quiet their minds, to reduce the chaotic stream of endless voices that plague them in the midst of mania or depression.

Bipolar or not, we each have moments when something sticks in the head and starts spinning 'round and 'round in there—and we can't seem to stop it. For the bipolar, this is a fairly common occurrence. Mark calls it "hamster-on-the-wheel" thinking.

When it does happen to you or to the bipolar in your life, try breathing in through the right nostril and out through the left nostril (remember, without using your hands). This requires an amazing amount of mental effort to accomplish, and the very concentration on making it happen tends to dissipate the spinning thoughts.

Remember, it is not always medication that works best. Sometimes it's little things like controlled breathing or meditative calming, things we can teach ourselves that are as effective in giving back control of the minds and thoughts as any medicine. Meditation in all its forms can be of tremendous help in allowing you to maintain your sanity and to help your bipolar maintain composure, as well.

The important thing for all of us is to *not* play inside our heads often or for long, but when we do, to know how to get ourselves out—breathe in, breath out.

Another form of meditation is known as "single point meditation," a technique in which you look deeply into a candle flame or at a formless object like a white-board. Often in this meditative modality there is chanting, rhythmic drumming, or praying via a single "sacred" word or phrase. Praying in this fashion is called a mantra or sutra. The word mantra literally means the *instrument of the mind.* Repeating a mantra slowly, over and over, produces a mental vibration and, when spoken or vocalized, also affects a soothing sound through the ears. Try the word "Om" or "so-hum". If you say them aloud, speak them slowly, at medium volume, each time stretching out the "m" sound for several seconds, at least. The sound will be something like this (take a deep breath and exhale slowly, saying): "Ommmmmmmmmmmmmm."

Either mantra is designed to clear the mind with a vibration. If you breathe in through your nose and think the word "So," and then breathe out, and think the word "Hum", you will produce a vibration that has been used for thousands of years in meditation.

A sutra is a mantra that has meaning. It has a related Latin noun, *suture,* which means *"to join together by sewing."* By using a mantra you can achieve a deeper level of consciousness, and by using a sutra you can place an intention into your mind.

For example, Mahatma Gandhi said, "Om Sir Rama, Jaya Rama, Jaya Jaya Rama" for 60 years of his life. This is a Sanskrit sutra that means: Om *(God sound)* Sir *(and)* Rama *(self-within)*, Jaya *(victory)*; so, translated, ***"And to the self-within, victory, victory to the self-within."*** I would imagine that Gandhi must have thought that by having victory over his own ego, he would be able to achieve more in his life. Considering his accomplishments, he must have been onto something. For more information on Sutra, turn to the Web Page Links listed in the back of this book.

I believe that if you ask for the way that is right for you, you will be led to it. That is why there are so many teachers on the subject. Dr. Wayne Dyer has an excellent tape on meditation that leads you through the process and contains both instructions and practice meditation sessions, some with music, others with chanting.

Whenever Mark and I bring up this subject in our support groups, the first question usually is, "How long does this take?" The answer we give is that sometimes it begins to produce a positive effect within just a few moments, and sometimes it can take an hour. The main thing is, don't give up— know and trust that it will happen.

Sometimes you will make the time to meditate and sometimes you will not. Don't be discouraged. This inconsistency happens to most of us—it seems to be a function of our busy lives. When we want meditation's benefits badly enough, though, a shift in our minds takes place—and it happens. There will be a moment when peace washes over you. Or you may suddenly, instinctively, *know the answer* to a question that you have asked. Don't be alarmed when this happens, it's supposed to.

Through mindfulness you can learn to stop the hamster-on-the-wheel kind of continuous thinking. You can create a gap in which to achieve beneficial meditation. Through meditation you connect with your Higher Power and tap into the healing energy that is there for all us. Mindfulness, meditation and affirmations will bring emotional peace and help you to survive, and the calmness it brings will help you recharge.

Use affirmations

"One drop of gratitude brings forth an ocean of abundance."

Affirmations are not just positive expressions; they are valuable tools for changing your cognitive thinking and your life. What we think and say, we believe. We are creating thoughts and beliefs all of the time—which is, of course, what choice is all about.

For example, you may be thinking, "I have no money to pay my bills; this is terrible; I am so miserable . . ." or whatever story you tell yourself.

As Dr. Phil says, "Is this working for you? Is this working for your relationships?"

I guarantee that we reap what we sow, or—better said—there is *a law of cause and effect*. Our thinking affects our actions as well as our thoughts. Now, you can choose to keep your negative thoughts and actions, but if you do, don't ask why the same negative things keep happening to you again and again. If you don't believe me, just ask your friends. I'm sure that they have heard the same story from you time and time again.

Changing your thinking is about changing your life! Changing your patterns and your reactions changes the outcome of your situation. It may not happen overnight, but I'll bet that if you start today, it will happen in about 21 days. As we all know, it takes 21 days to change a habit or behavior. Start today.

I grew up in poverty. My grandmother raised me on $450.00 per month, plus $50.00 worth of food stamps each month. The messages I grew up with were: "People will not help you, money does not grow on trees, life is hard, it's all about scratching and clawing your way to the top."

None of these messages have served me well, so as an adult I have chosen to change them. If I get an unexpected bill, I now say, "God must have more money planned for me to pay this," or "I am a money magnet, money comes to me"— and I always prosper.

Now, you may be saying to yourself, "But what if . . . ?"

I want you to know that in 43 years I have never **not** had a home to live in or food to eat. There have been many struggles, and all of my whining and complaining **never** made them any better. *In the negative thinking state, I was never able to find the right solutions, or answers.* Maybe that is because the Spirit is drawn to the light and to the positive.

So, how do you create an affirmation? Start with what the problem is, and then begin to think of what you want. Next, create a statement that you repeat every morning and night.

Let's take a common problem such as, "My home is crazy and chaotic." The affirmation would be something like, "Everything in my home is peace and love."

Here are just a few of the affirmations that I use:

- ♦ God is my source and my supply
- ♦ I always prosper
- ♦ I am a money magnet, money comes to me, people love to give me money and gifts

- The right people and situations always find me
- My business moves forward easily and effortlessly
- Mark and I have an intimate, loving sexual relationship (I wanted to cover everything)
- I have absolute faith that whatever I need is flowing to me now
- I have faith, trust and acceptance (this is the hardest for me)
- I release you to your life path

There are many books that deal specifically with affirmations. The one I have found to be the most help is *Life: Reflections on Your Journey*, by Louise Hay.

Dialectical Behavioral Therapy (DBT)

Dialectical Behavioral Therapy DBT) was developed by Professor Marsha M. Linehan, Ph.D., of the University of Washington Psychology Department for the treatment of Borderline Personality Disorder, a condition that research reveals affects 40% of all bipolars (research continually shows that in addition to their Bipolar Disorder most bipolars will have some other personality disorder, be it obsessive-compulsive or anxiety-based).

DBT therapy is a form of Cognitive Behavior Therapy that was designed to restore emotional regulation to patients. In Dialectical Behavior Therapy, the "dialectics" address conflicting demands and wants, and "behavior" refers to having strategic goals that you constantly compare to your actions. DBT assists you to better regulate your emotions to serve your goals, help your feelings of fear, increase your sense of personal identity, improve your judgment, sharpen your observation skills, and reduce the sense of crisis and chaos in your life.[2]

DBT is ideally suited to help those with mixed anxiety and depression because it offers interventions designed to treat the emotions themselves. Both depression and anxiety involve processes that make the patient overreact to threat signals and under-react to safety signals (the fight or flight response). DBT thus offers interventions to help challenge negative self-evaluation and allow more strategic control over variables in your environment.

Most bipolars and Personality Disorder patients deal with living and being in what Professor Linehan calls "Emotional Mind." Being in Emotional Mind is what spurs most romantic novels, and it explains why a mother will run into a burning building to save her child. It is not the kind of thinking that

---

[2] From Depressed & Anxious: The Dialectical Behavior Therapy Workbook, Thomas Marra

you want to be doing when you balance your checkbook or build a house. That sort of thinking is "Rational Mind" or logical thinking. Engineers use the rational thinking process, as do engineers, accountants and computer programmers. All of them get their jobs (and often their lives) done by applying this kind of thinking. The balance to these two minds is "Wise Mind." Wise Mind is the mental state in which we find peace, inner quietness, and (some would say) the spirit. You usually recognize instinctively the kind of person who has this aura about them. Think, for example, of a Buddhist monk. I believe that there are many other good examples, as well.

The next step in the DBT process is to achieve emotional regulation, and finally to learn the core skills for positive interpersonal relationships.

Two workbooks for this process have been published. One is a training guide for practitioners, and the other is a workbook for people who suffer from depression and anxiety. They can be ordered on the Internet or at any bookstore (reference to both books can be found in the Recommended Reading list in Appendix 1 at the back of this book).

There is a questionnaire, "Is DBT for You?" in Appendix 5 that you can use to determine whether you or your partner could use the DBT approach.

I will add here that this course was great for me. Again, when I am centered, Mark can stay grounded better, and practicing the DBT course together keeps us on the same page.

The example that I often give in workshops is that when someone used to cut Mark off in traffic, he would always take it personally and would say, "What's up with that guy? What's wrong with him?" to which I would respond, "Well, I'm sure out the six million people here in Phoenix, he chose you to make mad today, found your name in the phone book, looked up your address, and followed you around town to make your life miserable." The first time I said this, Mark first looked stunned and then bust out laughing. Once he began to practice not making up a story about the person that cut him off, Mark was able to *not* react verbally to the incident and remain in a positive space.

The DBT work is a structured course that takes about a year for the bipolar or borderline to complete, but for the non-bipolar, the workbook can be completed in about 12 weeks, and I would highly recommend studying it in a small group setting or with a friend.

Doing
What
Works

Be willing to change

The essence of insanity is doing the same thing over and over and expecting different results.

If the medication isn't working, the therapist isn't progressing, or the relationship is struggling—make some changes!

But what if the changes you make don't work? Better for them not to work than to do nothing and become angry and resentful. Try and try again to find something that does work, and remember, for most people it takes 21 days to change any habit, so be patient and give your change strategies time to work.

Many of us live in fear of change, so we do nothing and then wonder why we are not happy. Fear will keep you paralyzed in your present situation. I know this from personal experience. How to get past the fear? Think outside the box. Ask your therapist for ideas. Get a life coach. Remember, a coach or therapist can usually see the forest as well as the trees, and treatment professionals are not emotionally connected to your outcomes, so they have the ability to see more clearly than you can.

After I starting attending Al-Anon meetings, I chose a "sponsor"—a program member I felt I could relate to and trust—and I told her that I could no longer live as I had been living and that I would do whatever she told me to do! You see, I came to believe that I no longer had all the answers, and I knew that there was a better way, that *I just had to break out of the mold I had created*. So I read the books she recommended (about thirteen books in six weeks—I did not fool around) and I kept a journal on gratitude. I changed my "stinking thinking" and began to place affirmations all over my house, most of which are still there to this day. As a result of my sponsor's suggestions and my willingness to comply, my life and the lives of my family have been deeply changed, and for that I will always thank Spirit for my sponsor's presence in my life. There are no accidents; when a teacher is needed and you surrender, one will be provided for you.

This willingness to change implies that *together* you and the bipolar in your life will work to find mutually satisfactory solutions to problems, situations and triggers. As you work in partnership, communicating, deciding upon and implementing a plan, you will create an environment in which each of you will play a positive role in the relationship and thus will reinforce your mutual commitment to its success. This commitment keeps the bipolar's mind focused on recovery and keeps you grounded. Emotion and chemicals, often out of control and always adjusting to new/old triggers and situations, drive the world of the bipolar. In this dynamic environment it is important that you be able to embrace change and adjust your reactions and thoughts to changing, evolving situations. Not only are communication and the willingness to change the bases of any healthy relationship, they are even more so in the world of the bipolar.

Learn as much as possible

"Knowledge," wrote Sir Francis Bacon, "is power." Understanding Bipolar Disorder, being up-to-date about current medications, contemporary therapeutic methods, medical and non-medical alternatives, and current trends in treatment and recovery helps us work closely with our doctors and enables us to be proactive in Mark's recovery and treatment. Bipolar Disorder is a serious illness that requires you, as the non-bipolar, to spend a lot of time studying this illness. Read, search the Internet, talk with others—learn as much as possible. Ask your doctor to keep you informed about the "standard treatment protocols".

Know which mood stabilizer is the doctor's first choice (Lithium and Lamictal are currently the preferred drugs of choice for mood stabilization).

Find out why the doctor chose the drug he/she prescribes. Read up on the latest research for the drugs that are available and in current use.

Here are a few more questions you should ask:

- ◆ How many times a week or month does he want lab tests?
- ◆ What does he do for depression or mania? And why?
- ◆ If there is a problem with the medication over a weekend, do you call his office or do you go straight to the hospital?

By studying this illness you will gain insight into what others are doing to deal with it, which will make you better able to develop tools to help in your specific situation. By understanding medication options and side effects, you can better monitor the impact of the medications on your bipolar partner. Over time, the effectiveness of medications wears off because the body adjusts to the medications and they gradually lose their effectiveness. Mindfulness and open channels of communication with your bipolar partner will help you catch any change in behavior that might indicate that a change in medication or dosage should be explored. However, this awareness will only help to the extent that you become educated and informed.

Plan on several therapists

We saw several doctors and therapists before finding the right treatment professional. But almost as soon as we located him and started to become comfortable with him, he had a heart attack and we started looking again.

The choice of a therapist is one of the most important things you will do. The process of choosing must involve both the bipolar and the spouse, partner or family member. If either or both of you don't like—or have confidence in—the therapist, it will make the therapy process almost impossible.

Approach the selection process as though you are looking for a team member, someone with whom you can easily talk, a person who is committed to your treatment and with whom you can spend several years.

It is not uncommon to have *both* a medication doctor for the chemical imbalance and a therapist to develop the behavior and coping skills necessary to deal with this illness. Also, bear in mind that whether you are paying for services or receiving them through welfare, you must remain in control of the process. If either the doctor or the therapist is not meeting your needs or listening to what is happening with you, get up, shake their hand, and move on to the next practitioner on your list.

Your first meeting with a treatment professional is nothing more than an interview. Use the time well. Take a prepared list of questions with you, and don't be afraid to ask them directly and forcefully. You might consider some of the following:

- What experience with Bipolar Disorder do you have?
- Are you open to trying a variety of medications and closely monitoring their effectiveness?
- What have they learned in the last few months about Bipolar Disorder?
- What is your success rate in treating the other personality symptoms that accompany Bipolar Disorder?
- Will you meet separately with me (the non-bipolar) to evaluate my bipolar's progress?
- Are you available 24 hours a day in case of emergency? If not, what are the backup proced-ures?
- Do you know, understand, and use Dialectal Behavior Therapy in your therapy practice?

Finding a therapist—a good one—can be a daunting task. It is time consuming, incredibly frustrating—and absolutely necessary.

We have found that Interfaith Councils have been a big help, as have the Psychology Departments at many major universities. If you use a council or a non-profit social service agency, ask how they screen their therapists. Your medication doctor can usually provide referrals to area therapists, as well. And don't forget, you can get good information about treatment professionals from the members of your support group. In addition, you will find that many of the books written about Bipolar Disorder will also contain information and practical ideas for finding a therapist or doctor.

Once you have a doctor and a therapist, you should provide each of them with a medical release that will enable each of them to talk to the other. If your therapist sees you and you are in either a manic or a depressive state, he can then call your physician, and a plan of action can be formed right away so that the depression or mania can be arrested before hospitalization is needed. If you should change doctors, *be sure to get copies* of your records from the doctor you are leaving and pass them on to your new doctor. From time to time, it is also a good idea to get copies of your doctor's/therapist's notes for your own records.

Finally, if you are seeing a marriage counselor, *make absolutely sure* that he or she is experienced in dealing with Bipolar Disorder and related mental health issues.

Our first therapist highly recommended marriage counseling, which was wonderful, except that we chose a counselor who wasn't sensitive to the unique issues we were facing as a result of Mark's bipolar status. Mark would step into his calm and well-ordered "Dr. Jekyll" persona and everything would be fine, leaving our counselor confused as to what was going on. Only when "Mr. Hyde" finally showed up for a therapy session did she finally understand that I wasn't the problem and that we were facing issues greater than simply hitting a "bump" in our marriage. Depression and mania are *always* unreasonable, and until she could see Mark in his full form, she had no idea what I was facing. Mark always had a "good story" on how I just needed to get onboard and should be more positive in life. It sounded great to the counselor and, of course, she always wanted to know "why" I was not being positive. When I explained to her that we were $40,000 dollars in debt and Mark had no job, she assured me that the situation would soon change and that every marriage had financial problems occasionally. As I continued attempts to explain that the money was not the only problem and that he had what I at the time called "Peter Pan thinking." It was not until after he was diagnosed and *medicated* that our "marriage problems" all but disappeared. Needless to say, we immediately sought out a new therapist.

Meet with the therapist

When we started in therapy, I always met with the therapist after Mark's sessions. Now I meet together with Mark and the therapist in addition to meeting with the therapist alone.

This functional separation was critical in the beginning. Remember, if your bipolar is depressed, he or she will naturally become illogical and unreasonable, and, if manic, the bipolar can have an unrealistic positive attitude about every issue. By your meeting with the therapist you can provide a clearer picture of your situation at home, how the disorder is manifesting itself, and what situations are problematic.

Can you remember what upset you on day three or who triggered you on day five of the past seven days? More often than not, with effort and prodding, you can remember the past week. This isn't necessarily true for your bipolar partner or family member, and here's why that is significant. The bipolar will generally see the therapist once a week. For most bipolars, particularly if they have been cycling, trying to remember what happened even one day ago can be difficult or impossible. Often, we find that Mark has no memory of events that are only a day old.

My meetings with "Our Therapist" allowed me, with a less clouded memory, to fill in the blanks and give the therapist a more accurate picture of events, thus allowing both of us to be more productively proactive in helping Mark in his recovery.

At other times, my visits would ensure that Mark would remember the things he had been told to do and the issues he needed to address. Early on, the therapist made it very clear to Mark that he would be telling me what Mark's "assignment" would be for the week ahead. If Mark remembered, that was great, and if he did not, the therapist wanted to know that, too.

Another powerful reason for you, the non-bipolar, to visit regularly with the therapist is that you need someone who can coach you, who understands your situation, and who can help you stay sane and grounded. I cannot say it enough: it is not easy living with a bipolar, and your emotional well-being can take a beating. To think that you can live in the bipolar world without a personal therapist guiding you, giving you support, and helping you take care of yourself is simply unwise.

By any measure, the therapist will become one of the most important people you will know. The support and advice you will receive from this source will have an enormous impact on your life.

You need to meet with the therapist and build a strong relationship, just as the therapist needs to get to know you. I assure you, this "team approach" will prove to be incredibly valuable in terms of the bipolar's recovery, your sanity, and the peace of mind of your whole family.

Therapy for the non-bipolar

Therapy for the non-bipolar is about being "shorn up."

I had spent months questioning my own sanity and had walked around confused, either blaming myself or pissed off, thinking, "I'm doing my part! When is Mark going to do his?" For more than a year I had heard (and believed) that I "made him depressed" and that he was "never depressed before he met me." All of that was untrue, of course, but it was Mark's absolute reality at the time.

I also needed to know when it was "the illness talking" and not Mark. The therapist was consistently able to see the forest for the trees when I could not. Input from the therapist helped reduce the labeling and blaming that I was doing, and made me accountable when I needed to be accountable, and allowed me to release what was no longer true.

Time and time again, I had to be told by the therapist that Mark's illness had nothing to do with me, and that I needed to own that and make it my truth! When that principle sunk in, and it only took a couple of months, I began to trust myself. *Only* then was I able to be a team player for Mark.

The therapist needed a good, solid, rational perspective on the events that triggered Mark and made him unstable. I was a critical player in providing that perception, as he could not see what was happening to Mark at the time. It also gave me someone with whom to practice my new communication skills. When you practice with a friend or family member, that person tends to be "nice." You really need somebody who makes it challenging enough for you so that your skills continue to improve.

Our first therapist had the ability to push all my own buttons, hold me to a higher standard and expect me to recover in conversation, which is what I wanted and needed.

Both Mark and I believe and know now that therapy is one of the reasons why Mark has made so much progress and our marriage has become so much stronger.

Anger

"Resentment is like
sitting across the table from someone,
lifting your glass,
taking a big drink of a deadly poison,
and expecting the other person to die."

Debra Meehl

Another way of seeing resentment is as *"anger at a slow boil;"* the anger is always just beneath the surface, ready to explode.

I am asked many times how I managed to stop being angry and resentful. One way that I "chose" was to focus on Mark's positive attributes and to recall the reasons why I married him in the first place. The other path opened up almost by accident (of course there are no accidents). I had asked a prayer partner to pray that Mark and I could heal our marriage. Her only question for me was, "Are you willing to do whatever it takes to make this happen?" I immediately felt the fear in my throat! But my reply, through my tears, was, "It is too painful for me not to." You see, I was and still am just crazy about him. And in the weeks that followed, there were miraculous changes for us both.

Anger and resentment will eat away your relationship and rob you of any chance of finding loving moments together that are good for the two of you. My surrender and the subsequent diminishment of my anger and frustration did not mean that I was living in denial about our situation, it just meant that I chose acceptance over anger. As a result, problems became opportunities for growth and learning.

Oh, there were situations with finances, careers, and emotions that were not going to change overnight. And no amount of throwing myself around, needing to be right, would make things change any sooner. But eventually, with continuing effort on my part and with the support of the therapist, my attitudes gradually softened and changed, and every situation became better.

If you have decided to make a commitment to your relationship, and I would say that a minimum commitment should be at least six months, resolve also to release your past hurts and anger. Relief does not come overnight, but it does happen.

Pay attention

Pay close attention to changes in your bipolar's mood, demeanor and body language. Being mindful and aware of subtle changes enables you to manage and influence situations, perceptions and triggers, thus maintaining balance and calmness in your life. Awareness is critical if you are to maintain a mutually supportive home environment and have calmness in your life.

Mark's body language changes as he starts to feel "off," as he says. A characteristic scowl appears on his face. As soon as I notice this change, I respond. "You look like you don't feel well; are you OK?" Mark then does his own body assessment and usually agrees that there is something wrong, and we then begin looking for the trigger.

When problems occur and escalate, the chaos that follows often stems from a failure by either the bipolar or the partner to learn to pay attention to body language cues.

Communication skills: S.E.T. Communication

Have you ever had a conversation with someone during which you begin to think, "Are we talking about the same thing? Have I lost my mind here?"

When a bipolar is unstable, this is exactly what you will be thinking as you engage in conversation. Good, clear communication is the key to any successful relationship and is critical when a bipolar is involved.

There is no question that stable, fulfilling relationships are based on good communication. Bipolar Disorder often takes away a person's ability to reason. The bipolar becomes unreasonable, irrational, illogical and self absorbed. (See the depression chart in the back of the book.)

We believe in the use of SET (Support, Empathy, Truth) Communication. A bipolar will not hear the truth until he receives support and empathy for what he is thinking and feeling. He will perceive that you are not listening to him or don't understand him. And remember, just as we have the right to feel the way we feel, so does the bipolar.

Here is a typical conversation:

> **Non-bipolar:** "Honey, have you taken your medication today?"
>
> **Bipolar:** (yelling): "I hate it when you ask me that; don't ever ask me that me again!"
>
> **Non-bipolar:** "I understand that you feel this way. (*support*) It must make you angry. (*empathy*) but you have forgotten to take your medication several times before, and you went into crisis. (*truth*) Is there anything I can do to remind you without making you angry?"

Learn how to ask questions, how to explain what you are saying or hearing, and how to de-fuse any trigger. Communication will lead to **Mindfulness.** This conscious process will allow you and the bipolar to discuss what is happening when he is triggered, to find out what has caused him to be triggered, and to discover which situations to avoid (or at least to diminish the impact of) in the future.

Here is another example:

> **Bipolar:** "You don't love me any more"

Non-bipolar: "I am sorry that you feel that way." (*support*) "That must feel terrible." (*empathy*) The truth is, I do love you very much." (*truth*)

This approach can be taken with any confrontation or in any situation. There is no doubt that it takes a lot of practice. My first reaction used to be to always say something like, "That is the biggest load of crap I have ever heard." Although I felt immediate gratification, it didn't help the situation at hand. It was really hard to validate Mark's feelings about anything. I had to learn to respect his feelings even if in that moment I did not understand them or they made no sense to me.

The other thing I learned was to ask questions such as, "When did you first decide that I no longer loved you?"

There is always a trigger, and you must find it and deal with it. With both of you on board, being watchful and mindful, you can start the investigation into where the trigger is and what is causing it. Questioning is the only way to find it.

The last very effective tool that I learned was to be concise and direct.

I no longer say, "Do you want to go out tonight?" I now say things like, "Do you want to go to a movie, or to dinner, or both?" If I have an agenda for something, I do not play 20 questions, I just get right to the point. *This is also true for arguments—stay on the topic.*

The other day, Mark and I were in the car—he was driving—and I was upset that for the third week in a row the local newspaper had not printed a notice of our weekly support group. Mark had even gone down to their office and asked them directly to run the item. He was assured that they would do so. When the newspaper came out and it was not there again, I was angry and I said so. Mark immediately thought I was angry with him, but this time he just pulled the car over, looked directly at me and asked, "Are you angry at me for this?"

"Of course not!" was my reply. "How could this be your fault?"

"I thought maybe you thought there was something more I could have done."

"No, I never thought that."

"O.K."—and were back on the road again.

A year ago he would have blown up and been mad for days.

Another thing that has changed over the last year is that Mark is able to say that he is sorry, to which my reply is always, "Thank you." Period. Not "Thank you, what were you thinking?" Not "Thank you, let's hash out the subject again." Just a plain, simple, clear "Thank you." I get a lot more "I'm sorry" this way, as does Mark. By being concise and direct, we manage to avoid unnecessary confrontations or hurt and are able to get on with our life sooner.

When bipolars are raging and angry, they do not have a lot of verbal control, and often they experience dissociation, which is to say that later they cannot remember the event. Often, they report, it feels as though they are out of their own bodies and can only remember bits and pieces of what has happened or of what they have said.

It used to take days for Mark to say that he was sorry. He admits that he always felt like he had "egg on his face" or that he was "eating crow." Bipolars usually have a problem with low self-esteem, anyway. It is important that you be gracious when your bipolar expresses sorrow or remorse. If you need to talk about the event afterward, consider talking to the therapist first, and only then asking for mediation with your bipolar if it is necessary. Otherwise, drop it. Leave it alone. This is not the time to get your pound of flesh!

And if your bipolar is angry and walks away from you, there is a reason. Do not be like the yapping Chihuahua that everyone wants to kick. Leave your partner alone; enough is enough; you can always revisit the subject later if necessary. It does no good for either of you to provoke the other.

Good communication encourages a partnership in dealing with the impact of the bipolar's mood swings and through the process of discovering solutions. It increases both parties' understanding of what is happening and helps to provide better, more accurate information to your doctors. If communication is a challenge, work with your doctor and therapist to develop communication tools that you both can use, and attend a couples' retreat that deals with communication issues and offers a forum in which you can practice together in a safe and supportive environment.

Addictions

An addiction can be defined as *the willingness to give up everything to continue engaging in some particular (usually damaging) behavior.*

I will add here that a person will only stay in pain until it becomes too great, at which time they are driven to stop the pain. Most of the time, the "addiction" is something that changes the chemical balance of the brain, which is why most bipolars have had problems with some form of substance abuse—alcohol, drugs or some other substance, or "risky" behavior. The difference between abuse and addiction is that the definition of an addiction is the "willingness to give up everything to do it, while abuse by definition is *the improper or wrong use of something.* I say this so that no one jumps off a bridge when his or her loved one takes drugs or looks at a porn site. Depressed people are trying to find out

IF they can feel anything. Their *lack of ability to feel any emotion* is called Anhedonia, and it is a serious condition that often leads people to resort to cutting themselves to test whether they can feel pain.

As an example: a wife steps into her bipolar husband's study and catches him looking at a pornography web site on his computer. That could be immensely frightening or threatening to the wife, especially if the sex between the couple has waned lately. This is the point at which non-threatening and non-judgmental communication is most important. Screaming, yelling and crying, "How could you do this to me?" is not going to help and, in fact, will make it worse. "Why are you doing this?" is not going to help, either. Both of these questions only produce guilt, shame and defensiveness, not to mention that the bipolar husband now feels trapped, caught with his hand in the cookie jar, which is never a good way to start a conversation.

Remember that there are times when the bipolar is *just trying to feel anything.* More often than not, this is not personal. So instead, try something like, "Wow, what a beautiful woman (man, goat or whatever) and walk away. Later on, or the next day, try something like, "Are things between us O.K?" When your partner asks you why, you can then say, "When I saw you on that site yesterday, it made me feel insecure (lonely, bad, unattractive) and I just wondered." *The key here is to ask questions, not to berate or demand.*

The latest research (2002) shows that 99% of all bipolars have had problems with an addiction at some time in their lives[3]. Is it any wonder that they try to escape the pain or emotional void they are facing? This having been said, we believe that if your partner has a strong propensity toward any addiction, you should seek ways to help your bipolar to avoid the temptation. Of course, you should address the issue with your therapist, but do not jump to conclusions. Allow the professional to do behavior testing to see if, in fact, that there is an addiction. Seek the support of others through support groups and, if necessary, start a recovery program. If the problem is alcohol, don't leave five bottles of whiskey on the counter and then wonder why your loved one is drunk. If it is cocaine, don't have a line out on the table when your partner gets home, and if it's women, don't encourage your beloved to work in a bar.

You must treat the addiction, if for no other reason than that Bipolar Disorder is caused by a chemical imbalance in the brain. A chemical addiction of any sort

---

[3] Kessler & Walers. In: Tsuange and Tohen, eds, *Textbook of Psychiatric Epidemiology* 2nd ed., 2002

only serves to worsen the problem for the bipolar—and for you.

In the search for wellness, both you and the bipolar in your life must avoid addictions to the best of your ability and remain mindful of temptation. Start a dialogue, and involve your therapist as you discuss possible solutions.

We understand that this is a very difficult and sometimes painful path, but in this case you really don't have a choice if you have chosen to live healthily in the bipolar world and are hoping for any form of recovery.

Learn the triggers

For a bipolar, any subject or thought (conscious or unconscious) that reminds him or her of a trauma or causes so much discomfort that an emotional reaction occurs is a "trigger." Triggers can occur when a bipolar sits down to pay the bills, talks about childhood, thinks or talks about negative past job experiences, deals with tense situations with the family or as the result of any number of issues, some of which would seem minor to anyone else.

These triggers can cause the bipolar's palms to sweat, stomach to ache, or head to explode into a migraine-like headache.

Triggers are insidious; they can be as simple as a word, a tone of voice or a phone call. Once triggered, the bipolar mind begins racing and thoughts become chaotic. Suddenly, it feels like a thousands lights going off all at once, each producing a thought, an argument, or an answer as entire internal dialogues take over, drowning out everything else.

If you're a bipolar, triggers are not necessarily caused by bad things in your life or by negative actions or statements. Strangely enough, success can also be a trigger, and it can make you so uncomfortable that self-sabotage begins immediately. If you have spent years living in a constant drama, things like peace, joy and harmony will feel so uncomfortable that you very well may unconsciously sabotage the success and happiness that is already in your life. If all this applies to you, know that you are not alone. Many bipolars are success-depleted; they have cycled so many times that it can be difficult for them to bask in the sunlight of success rather than to constantly wait for the other shoe to drop—or simply to throw it out the window, thus creating chaos in the midst of calm.

Healing and sanity for the non-bipolar truly lies in becoming mindful and aware. It is at this point that therapy truly can work miracles in both your life and the life of your bipolar family member as you seek to reduce the impact of triggers.

By using therapy to help identify the triggers (subjects/causes) that set the bipolar off, you can either consciously avoid them or develop a plan to minimize the damage if a trigger sets off an episode. Through the communication and awareness that therapy can facilitate, you and your bipolar can learn to discuss triggers as they occur, and together you can develop a plan for breaking the hold of the trigger and reducing its impact.

Look at the obvious trigger and then begin digging for the real trigger.

Mark actually draws out the trigger on our bathroom mirror, like this:

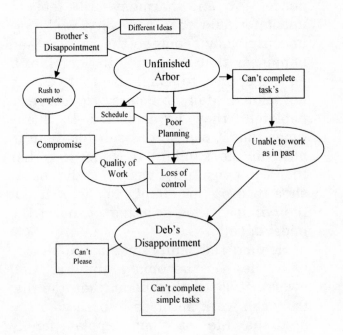

Using dry erase pens, he uses boxes and arrows to isolate what the trigger is and then works out why it is a trigger. From there, he looks at the *whys*, and *whys* of the *whys*, until together we figure out what in the world the real trigger is.

Once you know what the trigger is, you can overcome it and, as Mark says, "kill it," or at least learn how to minimize its impact on both of you.

Mark has discovered a number of triggers that will set him off. The challenge is to be able to determine if the trigger is related to his Bipolar Disorder or something else.

As an example, Mark and his brother, who was visiting with us, set out to build an arbor along the full length of our house. It was a project that was to take about ten days, something to keep the men busy. The goal was to finish the project by the day before Mark's brother was to fly home. By dinnertime on that evening, the arbor was still not quite finished. Mark came in for a quick drink of water, only to find that I had managed to plug the sink with potato skins and that the disposal just could not handle them. He would have to clear the disposal. At another time, this would not have been a big deal for Mark, but as he plunged the sink he got madder and madder and madder until he started beating the sink faucet with the plunger, breaking the plunger handle and sending pieces flying everywhere. Later, when we were able to talk about it, we discovered that the incident had nothing to do with the sink or me, but it had everything to do with what he felt was the deep "disappointment" of not getting the arbor done in time—and what his brother would think of him—and how I would take it. The stress of the situation created itself entirely in his own mind and mushroomed until it exposed itself in the "beating" of the faucet.

Welcome to the world of triggers.

For a man who had lived through and thrived in stressful situations, Mark's Bipolar Disorder has, at times, taken away his ability to handle even the tiniest stresses. His frustration manifests itself in rage or depression and continues until we can find the trigger and determine why it is having an impact *now*. Will that particular stress be a problem from now on? Who knows—but by being mindful and aware of what is going on we can definitely reduce the number of triggers and mitigate their impact.

As we have emphasized already, these processes, mindfulness and awareness, allow us to set clear areas of responsibility in our daily life, to determine what "works" and what does not.

For instance, we have agreed that Mark will not talk on the phone when he is triggered. The phone has been known to set him off on many levels, so keeping him isolated from that known source of trouble reduces the potential for other triggers to develop as a result of a phone call, such as one from a telemarketer.

Incidentally, after Mark "went off" on the phone company when they called one day asking us to upgrade our service, we have not had any more solicitation calls from the phone company (which may not be such a bad thing).

Stopping the triggers:
a wholistic treatment plan

Teamwork: the process of finding common ground, meeting each other's needs, and knowing each other's limitations; this is the plan that you and your bipolar partner should agree upon at a time when you are both in balance.

You and your partner will first make a list of your root triggers, and you'll negotiate a plan for what you can/will do when *you or your partner* is experiencing irritation, rage or mania. This process should take several hours.

Journaling is the best way to do this kind of work, and it may take a therapist, a life coach, or a mediator to help you complete the list. Remember, the things that you see are not necessarily the ones that your partner will be willing or able to see. The first thing, then, is to keep it simple, at least for a while.

For example: If one of your bipolar's triggers is the lack of three meals a day and he or she becomes irritated when this happens, you—the partner—may want to speak out with a reminder that it is lunch time, or suggest going out to get a burger, or ask if you can fix something for your partner as you fix something to eat for yourself. If sleep is the problem, then maybe a more regimented sleep schedule is needed. If work is the main trigger and you are truly concerned about your partner's health, maybe not working for a while is the answer—or a career change may provide the answer. If housework is the problem, hiring a maid for two hours a week may be all the help that is needed, and the $20.00 a week it will cost might well be worth it to silence the constant yelling and arguing about whose turn it is to clean the house.

A treatment plan is a guide that is *clearly written down*, with an agreed-upon list of things that you and your partner are willing to do to make your relationship and your lives better.

Here is a list of a few things to try as ways to reduce the emotional response to triggers:

- ♦ Regular sleep times
- ♦ Regular, calming meals
- ♦ At the sign of irritation, no caffeine or spicy food
- ♦ Back rubs, hand or foot rubs, neck rubs
- ♦ Hot bath or Jacuzzi, with lavender oil

- ♦ Exercise - moderate
- ♦ Tea: chamomile or some other de-caffeinated tea
- ♦ Eliminate overtime at work
- ♦ Yoga
- ♦ Deep breathing
- ♦ Get a massage, a pedicure, or a manicure
- ♦ Light a candle at church
- ♦ Take a nap

All these are things that can be done immediately.

When Mark becomes irritated, it is most probable that he is over-stressed. This can happen with family or even with therapy. Often, Mark just takes a nap, allowing his brain to re-boot (much like a computer). I don't ask if he is depressed, angry or irritated, I just let it be, and usually he is able to communicate better after a nap. We can then discuss, in a calmer and more rational way, what triggered the emotional episode.

When confronted with raging

First, don't take anything personally. Next, read *The Four Agreements* by **Don Miguel Ruiz**. This book should be required reading for anyone living with a bipolar loved one. It is the one reading assignment we most often recommend to people in our support groups.

Both of us have read it and through it have found incredible peace and understanding, as well as discovering tools that each of us can use to keep calmness in our house and reduce the number and severity of some of the triggers that have plagued us in the past. The Ruiz book has also allowed us to dig deeper in discovering why Mark is triggered. The first three Agreements pertain to our situation, and here is a précis of Don Miguel Ruiz' text.

ৰ্ঠ

The first agreement is: **Be impeccable with your word.** Avoid using the word to speak against yourself or to gossip about others, and speak words only in truth and love. Speak in your mind and out loud with integrity.

This was the first step for Mark toward being mindful, not speaking against himself. He had to give up the "poor me," "I'm to blame," "I'm unworthy" thinking. That "old thinking" triggered emotions of helplessness, hopelessness or, worst of all, powerlessness, which usually threw him into depression. As he began to tell the truth about himself, he was better able to accept his limitations and rejoice in who he truly is.

The second agreement is: **Don't take anything personally.** What others say and do is a projection of their own reality and beliefs. And you can be immune to the opinions and actions of others. In the beginning, Mark took everything personally. He needed to please everyone at his own expense, and he believed what others thought of him. He was certain that he must have some serious personality flaw that made it impossible for him to please everyone all the time, and since he couldn't be everything for everybody, he created a different social mask for every occasion. The weight of that almost superhuman effort was a huge load to carry all of the time. Self incrimination brought about by "buying into" the opinions and actions of others will always produce triggers.

The third agreement is: **Don't make assumptions.** Be clear in what you really want to communicate, and communicate in a way that avoids drama, sadness or misrepresentation. Mark used to make assumptions about what I thought or about how dis-appointed I was *going to be* about something. Again, this had everything to do with how Mark was raised and had nothing to do with me. He released this idea once he believed that I would be truthful in talking about my feelings regarding things (see Agreement One).

২

We all seem to be conditioned to take things personally, to think everything is about us. Mark and I call this "me, me, me thinking." Most of the time, when people speak, it is about themselves—their ideas, beliefs, conditions and judgments—their talk seldom has much to do with us, their listeners.

I was so afraid of saying the wrong thing at the wrong time that the therapist actually asked me, "How does it feel to be God?" I was stunned! I was just trying to say the right thing. You see, I thought that if I could say the right thing 100% of the time I could prevent him from being triggered. But in reality it had nothing to do with me and everything to do with Mark's perception.

He let me know right then and there that Bipolar Disorder has absolutely nothing to do with me and that Mark would need to take responsibility for his emotions and reactions. Now, this does not mean that I was going to consciously try to invoke his triggers; it means that I had to stop walking on eggshells, constantly worried about triggering Mark.

I also had to remember that in the midst of raging, Mark wasn't sure himself of what he was saying and that he never remembered exactly what went on (this is called dissociation). At that point, my taking anything personally would serve only to make the situation worse. I needed to release my need to be right and/or to make him wrong. I needed to "detach with love" (another wonderful Al-Anon term) and understand that this, too, would pass. And, most of all, I needed to personally release any anger or resentment. After all, rational thinking should tell me that to take anything personally in such an interaction would be foolish, indeed, in light of the medical fact that whatever Mark might say it wouldn't be about me, it would simply be the product of a chemical reaction in his brain triggered by an event I probably had nothing to do with. His "stuff" in those moments was nothing more than his disease, Bipolar Disorder, *talking to him, not to me.*

Of course, there were some things I could choose to do to help, but the bottom line was—and still is—that *Mark is committed to recovery, and each episode is just his brain screwing with us.* That simple but profound insight has made it much easier for me not to take personally anything Mark says in the middle of raging or depression.

It also helps if I remind Mark—when he gets out of control—that there is a shovel in the trunk of the car and it's a big desert—they'll never find his body.

Now, I know what you are thinking: "Oh, my God, how could she say that!"

Actually, it's an inside joke that comes from a story I heard when I was working in a local hospital. Here is the story.

One afternoon, a lovely older couple came into the ER, and when I noticed how very attentive they were being to each other I commented on how nice that was and how good it made me feel. The husband responded that they had been married "forever" and that humor kept their relationship alive. In fact, the wife chimed in, telling me that on the way back from her first oncology appointment, on the day she learned that she had cancer, she told her husband that she was glad she had the cancer rather than he. Without skipping a beat, he replied, "Me, too." In an instant, mortified beyond belief as he realized what he had just said, he began to stammer . . . until, a few seconds later, she burst out laughing.

She then patted my hand and said, "I told him 'It's a big desert, they will never find your body.'" Then they both started laughing.

Before they left the ER that day, the husband whispered to me that his wife was "the love of my life."

I never doubted it for a moment.

Don't push back against rage

When confronted with rage, stand your ground, but do not push back. Reactive behavior will only inflame the situation further and make it worse. Backing up or walking away will also make things worse. *Affirm that you understand they are upset and that you care.* Stay on that message, repeating it over and over until you break through the rage.

In the midst of rage, there is no sanity. The bipolar's mind is racing out of control, the rage feeding itself with anger and frustration, escalating until either you break through or it burns itself out. To fight back, verbally or physically, will only fuel the rage. So stay on message and stand your ground. Be as gentle as you can, but remain firm, and remember this: never endanger yourself or your children; if the raging should turn violent, leave immediately and call the police.

The idea here is to defuse the mania or rage. Call the prescribing physician and explain the situation. Often a small, temporary change in medication is all that is needed to break the cycle. We obviously recommend that medication options for breaking the raging be discussed before they become necessary. If you have not done it yet, this is a conversation that should occur as a part of your next visit with both the medication doctor and the therapist.

This is extremely important because medication also breaks the cycle of behavior. As the bipolar rages, the brain's chemical balance is also out of balance, and as the rage continues you may also scream or throw things, and sometimes that serves to break the rage and the bipolar is fine once again.

The problem here is that *physically* violent behaviors can become *patterned* violent behaviors that are not desirable. Remember Pavlov's dog. As the bipolar's rage escalates, it becomes emotionally painful to experience internally, and the bipolar is driven to release it. Surely, punching the walls or throwing lawn furniture around the yard is not a pattern of behavior that anyone wants. Medication as needed can break the cycle. As an example in our lives, when Mark increases his Zyprexa dose (as indicated and recommended by his prescriber) for just one day, positive things happen. An extra 5mg dose will put him to sleep, his brain seems to re-boot, and he awakens feeling fine. Sometimes there's a bit of a medication hangover, but that's a small price to pay for the relief the medication adjustment brings—no mania and no rage.

This strategy may or may not work for you, but it is worth a try. However, ***never experiment with medications unless your prescribing physician knows about it and approves of it!***

Working with the therapist, you and your bipolar can develop meditations, mantras or prayers that you both can use to help break through raging and depression. Biofeedback techniques are often helpful, too. Our therapist hooked Mark up to a biofeedback machine, and we watched his responses while the therapist purposefully provoked him. I observed Mark's physical behavior as he went through the process. Then we all talked about what we had observed, and we made a plan of action to defuse the trigger in the future by using techniques such as deep breathing and muscle relaxation to reduce the adrenal overload.

Making an action plan, *together*, places the bipolar in perceived control of the treatment and helps to restore some of the lost self-esteem that Bipolar Disorder produces. Agreeing when medication and when behavior changes should be implemented, places you together on the same page. By making these agreements ahead of time, the bipolar will be less resistant to your actions when raging.

Zero tolerance

There must be ZERO tolerance for violence. There can be no hitting, no scratching, no verbal abuse. These are simply inexcusable and should not be tolerated. Bipolar Disorder is **not** an excuse for physical violence. Do not put up with it—call the police. The only time to fear the possibility of violence is when they are either in a manic state, or they believe it is acceptable. If it is the latter, give yourself credit—you deserve better. If it is due to a manic episode, the police (based on your mental health power of attorney) will take your bipolar to the hospital for care and medications. Will this enflame your bipolar? Probably, and you will have to decide whether or not you deserve to live with violence in your household. If you decide NOT to allow violence—set limits, make agreements and work together to maintain a non-violent house. Find an outlet for violent feelings by getting a punching bag, finding classes in kickboxing, buying a Nerf bat—find something that can be an outlet for the anger and rage. And change the medications to address the anger.

The damaging effects that violence inflicts on your health and that of any children in the household must not be tolerated. The emotional and physical scars can last for years and often take many more years of therapy to heal. Bipolar Disorder is a mental illness, not an excuse for violence. Being bipolar doesn't, in and of itself, make a person violent. Violence is a learned behavior, and if it is tolerated, it is reinforced. So:

- Change the behavior
- Identify the triggers
- Talk with your therapist
- Set limits
- Make agreements
- Keep them!

Your therapist can help identify the triggers, and your bipolar can learn to limit personal behavior and reactions.

You also need to work with the therapist to learn coping tools and ways to reduce anger and rage. One aspect of this is that the bipolar must stick to a commitment to therapy and medication that can control the anger and raging. For your part, you must stay true to the boundaries you set and the agreements you make.

Since violent outbursts and anger are usually controllable through medication, there is simply no "excuse" for violent behavior. If the medications don't stop violent outbursts, or at least allow the bipolar to control anger or rage to a noticeable degree, communicate with the doctor immediately and ask that adjustments be made in the dosage or that the medication be changed.

Finally, and a bit sadly, although we understand how difficult this situation can be, we firmly believe that you do not need and should not permit violence in your life. Either control it, medicate it, or get out and get on with your life.

Commitment to medication

The bipolar in your life must commit to taking the prescribed medications regularly and on time. If this means setting limits on the relationship, then so be it. For instance, you may need to have a temporary separation pending your partner's commitment to accepting the idea of taking medication. Neither of you can deal with this illness without medication. Many bipolars start a course of medication only to stop soon after because they feel so much better, not realizing that stopping will only produce a disastrous downward spiral into mania or depression, creating chaos while the bipolar insists the whole time, loudly, "Of course I'm taking my meds!" This is denial, not recovery. You will need to decide personally for how long and under what circumstances you are willing to live in chaos. Remember, your bipolar will need to have medications changed periodically, anyway, because not very many medications work all of the time. You are going to have periods of upheaval from time to time regardless of the treatment in effect, but you most certainly don't need to encourage chaos.

The issue of medication is far and away the leading cause of problems for the bipolar. It's all too easy for the bipolar, now feeling much better (thanks to the medications), to decide that medications are no longer needed. Yes, the ugly monster called "denial" can rear its head at any time, and the better your bipolar feels the more likely it is that he or she will want to take all the credit for success.

The bipolar, of course, wants more than anything else to be cured. When the medications have done their work, there may be an appearance of cure. The bipolar feels fine and looks fine, but it's an illusion, not a cure. This is where education and boundaries come into play—education from the doctor and the therapist, boundaries from you. Just as the insulin-dependent diabetic needs to continue to take insulin, so does the bipolar need to take appropriate medications—and continue taking them regularly.

Upon discontinuance of medication, it may be couple of days or even weeks before the bipolar again feels manic or starts to feel depressed, *but it will happen*.

Not only must your bipolar loved one make this commitment, but, if necessary, there must be an agreement between you that you must personally administer, or witness the taking of, every medication—at least for a while at the beginning. This strategy accomplishes two things: 1) if your bipolar suffers from forgetfulness it helps overcome the possibility of a missed dose; or an incorrect dose and 2) you will feel more secure.

Set a specific time of day or night to take the medications and hold to that schedule until it becomes a habit. If possible, take the medications at night, just before bedtime—this can help reduce some of the side effects during the day. Once a schedule has been established and followed until it's virtually second nature for the bipolar, you can ease off a bit by becoming not a monitor but a *gentle, occasional reminder—a partner.*

Another reason to become educated about medication and side effects is that if the medication makes the bipolar feel hung-over or if there is a sexual side effect, the bipolar most likely will not continue to take it. This all but makes medication commitment or compliance impossible. This concept is not rocket science! If the medication made you or me sick, we wouldn't take it, either. This is where your support and under-standing will also come into play. It usually takes about three weeks to know if a medication is going to work, and if it does not work, it will take another three weeks or so to test the next medication. Your encouragement in this process is crucial. Your partner may tell you that they feel like a "guinea pig" and that this is just not worth it. Reassure them that in the long run it will be well worth it and that they will function better as soon as the right meds are found. Remind him or her, too, that hospitalization is always an option. The average stay in the hospital is two to three weeks, just about the same time it takes to find the right combination of medication for mood stabilization. If the medication produces side effects that make the bipolar miserable, make an appointment right away with the treating physician. And before you embark on any new course of medication, be sure that you know and understand the possible side effects of the prescribed medication before the bipolar begins taking it.

Finally, if your bipolar has not taken his or her medication out of defiance, he or she will need to come to terms with the destruction and chaos that has happened in the wake of the illness. This is one of the ways that trust is restored in a relationship.

Once you have created a wholistic treatment plan there should be no confusion about what to do and when to do it, thus the chaos of any potential problems with medication will be reduced.

The medication stopped working

Oh, My God!

It happens—sometimes often. In some cases, the body simply adjusts to the medication or the dosage level, which is called medication tolerance. In other cases, medications may be sensitive to heat, either environmental or physical. Something as seemingly benign as catching a common cold or taking a cold medicine can interfere with a medication's effectiveness, and this loss of efficacy may produce mania.

Lithium dosage, for instance, generally needs to be adjusted during summertime in Arizona, where we live, because of the desert heat. If a bipolar drinks too much water, medication in the system, even though administered in "proper" dosage, may become diluted and may no longer work properly. At the other extreme, sweating will lead to dehydration, one result of which may be that the medication produces a toxic response.

A change in physical activity in any season can alter a medication's effectiveness, too, and may require an adjustment, depending on how much change there has been from normal and customary activity levels.

More often than not, unfortunately, a medication loses its effectiveness not so much because the body adjusts to it but because it may have been the wrong medication to begin with.

Because the situation is so quickly changeable and unpredictable, we stress that every bipolar and every family member who is affected by the bipolar needs to be mindful of what is happening and should learn as much as possible about the medications that are being prescribed, what other medications are available, the potential side effects of each possible choice, and most importantly, precisely what each medication is designed to do.

An informed family member often is better able to recognize when something is "not right." When that feeling arises, that's the time to talk to the your bipolar to check on what's happening. The first question always should be, "How are you feeling?" Then, "Is everything all right?" Tell the bipolar what you are observing—remember, what's going on in your mind and in the bipolar's mind are two very separate things. Remember, too, that this is a team effort, after all, and it should be perfectly OK for you to notice a change before the bipolar does.

In either case, note it in the daily journal and bring it to the doctor's attention. An adjustment in the medication or a change of prescription may be indicated.

You should expect that the medications will continue to change as the body adjusts, and you should also be alert to the release for sale of new medications and the advent of new treatments for Bipolar Disorder.

Crisis procedures

1. In most large metropolitan cities, there is a Crisis Hotline, staffed with a team of people who can evaluate a mentally ill person. The number of the local Crisis Hotline is one of those "must know numbers" to add to your address book, list in your computer and pin up on the family bulletin board. In the middle of a crisis there may be virtually no time in which to find the right number to call. Obviously,

if the situation is beyond the crisis stage, you can call 911 for the police.

2. When confronted with "I'm not going to the hospital," you will need to complete and file a form requiring a mental health evaluation. This form has various names, depending on your state of residence, but where we live, in Arizona, it is called a Title 36 form. It is the document you use to authorize that someone be taken to the hospital, whether voluntarily or not, for a psychiatric evaluation. There are three categories for a Title 36: Danger to others (DTO), Danger to self (DTS) or Persistent and Acute Disability (PAD). Most hospitals that have a behavior unit, and all police departments, can provide this form. The document needs to be filled out and signed by a judge before the police or an ambulance crew can pick up a patient. After normal business hours, you can still reach the police and they can lead you through any procedure needed to assure that your loved one receives treatment.

3. After a patient, in this case your bipolar, reaches the hospital, a qualified, credentialed therapist is required by law to evaluate the patient. The physician, usually a psychiatrist, then admits the

patient for a 72-hour evaluation, during which everyone on the hospital's evaluation team records observations of the patient, and from those notes and discussions a diagnosis is determined and the patient is then asked if they want to stay. They can either be admitted on their own or by court order for further treatment. If, in fact, they do need to be admitted for long-term treatment, the judge can then give a Guardianship to you.

Procedures and forms in every state differ, so learn about local, state and city procedures in your area ahead of time. Most hospitals with a behavior unit can tell you the procedure or your local police department or crisis Hotline.

Nurturing
Your
Relationship

Measurable progress

Regardless of the treatment modality or medication regimen your doctor and therapist prescribe, insist on measurable progress. If you can't see over time that your bipolar is improving, change therapists or doctors. In effect, you should "know" that every practitioner is dispensable until you find the right combination of treatment professionals, a "team," each of whom becomes a full partner in the recovery effort.

Insist on knowing the criteria your treatment "team" has established for measuring your bipolar's progress. Be certain you understand exactly what they see as progress and keep that "picture" in your mind so you can perceive and evaluate on your own.

Even with all this knowledge and understanding, don't expect the path of treatment to be smooth and free of "pebbles"—perhaps even some "big rocks."

For me, this understanding was one of the most important facets leading to my newfound ability to be calm and "cool" in the face of any of Mark's behavioral or attitudinal swings. It enabled me to recognize positive change as it occurred and to cope with any negative swings, and it gave me hope for the future even when the stresses and constant chaos of

Mark's illness were taking their toll on our relationship and family life.

We started with a daily mood chart (see the Appendix or go to the Meehl Foundation Website). We adapted our chart from several previously published evaluation tools, finally devising one that lists most of the common problems that crop up in Bipolar Disorder. We even left a few extra blank lines at the bottom for recording phenomena that others may not have acknowledged, or for unusual situations that seemed to be uniquely new to our experience at the time they occurred.

It was important that we both kept a chart of our own feelings about and our individual responses to Mark's bipolar behaviors. Remember, it's all about perception.

The next thing is journaling. This process doesn't have to be "fancy," with formal journal books and so forth. You can use a lined pad, a loose-leaf notebook, or a 'journal book' that you'll find in most local stationery stores. As for procedures, one page for each day will usually do, and you may write in prose, or in short, bulleted "lists," or even in poetry if that's your strong suit. Just write down what has gone right today and what is still going wrong, as well as what you are grateful for and what still needs to change. There are no rules, no formulas. All each of you really needs is an absolutely clear personal understanding—a *mindfulness*—about what is different today and how situations have evolved since yesterday, or last week, or last month, or last year. Write what you know, write what you feel, write what you think . . . in the end, it will show you, and your treatment professionals, who and where you are.

What is a sufficient interval within which to measure progress? We have decided to measure our progress in six-month increments. For us, any shorter time frame seems skewed by daily situations, short-term variables and temporary environmental or emotional conditions. The six-month time frame seems to allow us to average out and level off the short-term variables and to track the more gradual, longer-term progress we seek to measure.

In the approximately 18 months since we began this tracking process we have seen considerable progress. We can also spot the times when forward momentum was interrupted by something major, such as the two or three times when Mark's medication clearly needed to be adjusted or changed.

As we write this section, we have just come through a rather good month (in terms of general equilibrium), but that followed a prior month that was filled with various "disasters." On average, though, are we able to say—and see— that there has been measurable progress? No doubt about it—as long as we look at the whole picture. Looking back over the last six months and using our charting as a guide and a kind of "reverse road map," we see progress in communication, in identifying triggers, and in reaching or exceeding most of the goals we set for the time period. Our dating and bonding goals have really been realized. Most situations that were potential disasters for us just a few months ago are far less problematic today.

Over this period, we have tried hard to remember that when progress seems to be missing or unattainable, it's up to us to discuss the situation with our therapist and sometimes with our doctor, and to look with them for ways to continue moving forward.

Journaling

"Wisdom is already there;
it is a wave of expression."

Let's take a closer look at the journaling process to see how it can be helpful.

Journaling is one of the most revealing and rewarding techniques to use as a tool for growth for the bipolar and non-bipolar alike. Creating a self-care journal of activities and events that make you happy is one way to regulate emotions, calm the mind, and free the body of built-up emotional stressors.

Collect photos of nature, seasons, places, people, or anything that nourishes you.

Asking and answering questions in your journal is also helpful. You might consider writing about subjects such as:

- I have always wanted to

  _____

- The 10 things I am most grateful for today are:
  (<u>make a new list every day</u>).

- A nurturing place near my home is _____

- Things that I enjoy that don't cost money are:

  _____

- My favorite thing to do in bad weather is:

  _____

- The things I like about myself are:

  _____

- My best talents are:

  _____

- My spouse is great because:

  _____

One of the things that I like to do is collect flowers from the places to which we travel. Last week, I saw a pansy (they are my favorite to collect). I picked it and placed it in the book I was reading. Months from now, when I pick up that book again, I will be reminded of the trip. It will be a pleasant feeling. I also pick up pennies or other coins when I am walking about. I consider them gifts from heaven, and I am reminded that God is my source and my supply. Yes, I usually say it out loud. The other day Mark found a ten-dollar bill. What a gift!

Laugh

Laughter truly is the best medicine. There is more than enough evidence of the healing power of humor with respect to physical ailments, both in the clinical literature, in popular books and stories, and in our personal experience. Laughter can also be used to help someone break the grip of mental states like depression or mania.

The act of shared laughter is definitely valuable in terms of bonding. With this in mind, continually seek to find events or situations in the life of your bipolar that you can get him or her to laugh about. By the way, seeing the humor that underlies all of this can also help the non-bipolars in the family. Laughter is a great healer and will help all of you stay sane.

Mental illness is serious stuff and the struggle to deal with it on a daily basis can take a toll. If you take the time to be mindful, you will almost invariably find a vein of humor even in the midst of rage and depression. Deb is not beyond laughing at the words flying from Mark's raging mouth. Not only is this good for her, but it often starts to break through the mania by putting a more humorous light on everything. When faced with the stresses of mania or depression, do not lose sight of the healing power of laughter.

Having trouble finding things to laugh about? Keep a journal and then go back and read what you wrote. You'll likely discover something that you can at least smile about—if you try.

Some people keep a library of funny videos and collect humorous stories to hand to their bipolar when a situation indicates the need to really lighten up.

Intimacy

Sometimes I feel emptiness in my heart when I realize in a given moment just how much I love Mark and yet don't feel the loving connection that brought us together—that something vital is missing. I feel lonely and somehow distant from him, but the more I try to fill the emptiness, the more deeply I feel the void until it becomes a sort of black hole with no bottom. This is how the absence of emotional intimacy feels to me.

Bipolars in the midst of mania or depression are not capable of emotional intimacy. They are, in essence, emotionally unavailable.

True intimacy must have three components:

- *The relationship must be mutual*: each partner must have the ability to leave or stay. They must be able to choose to stay, and not out of guilt or shame. There should be none of that "I can't leave because he cannot make it without me" thinking or "he will kill himself if I don't stay . . ."

- *There must be reciprocal empathy*: it must be present on both sides of the relationship, meaning that both people are *willing to try to understand* the other's feelings and emotions.

- *There must be a balance of power*: no inequality here. Both partners must bring what they can to the relationship. The power is seldom if ever equal, but it cannot be too far out of balance or there will be great unhappiness and resentment.

So how can you achieve intimacy in your often troubled relationship?

Remember the boundaries that we emphasized at the beginning of the book? That's how!

You set boundaries so you have something to give to another rather than to be someone your bipolar can just take for granted and take advantage of whenever the occasion arises.

Boundaries are why my kids don't rummage in my purse, why my neighbor does not borrow my underwear, and why my husband does not use my toothbrush. It is also the reason that I do not have to be emotionally responsible for another person's thoughts, behaviors or emotions.

I usually hear about these issues from women—I think it's because their life conditioning makes them more easily able to express themselves verbally, so they know how to give voice to the fact that they just don't feel loved, or that they feel abandoned, or that they don't seem to be *connected!*

My standard reply is that they should check the three critical criteria that are bulleted above and find what is missing. Once they do this and make the appropriate course corrections for their relationships, the intimacy will return and their hearts will feel full again.

In summary, even though you will certainly encounter the problems, do whatever you can to fix them. Know that your situation won't resolve itself overnight. And while you are doing what you can, also begin rebuilding the relationship—consciously—using all the effective techniques of bonding, reconnecting and dating that I'm about to discuss.

Also, please note that I did *not* say that you are going to dump all of this on your partner and dictate what needs to be fixed. I said that YOU are going to find the problems and that you'll fix what you are able to fix. Believe me, when you do, your partner will notice, and at that point an open discussion will become possible and will very likely begin (which is a great step forward, right?)

If, after several weeks, your bipolar doesn't notice, be sure to discuss the situation with your therapist because there may be a larger problem.

Bonding and reconnecting

It is critical that you and your bipolar bond and reconnect in moments of calmness. In such moments, the simplicity of a touch conveys many things—understanding, affection, love and commitment—and yet, as easy as it is to do, it can be incredibly difficult to make these sorts of connections in the bipolar world. In the periods between depression and mania, the bipolar experiences many emotions, but the hardest and most painful ones are embarrassment, guilt and remorse.

Like many things in the bipolar world, you will need to learn new skills to handle many interactions that you used to take for granted. The act of touching can help alleviate these feelings in your bipolar and may also help you soothe the wounds and unintentional hurts that Bipolar Disorder causes. You, the non-bipolar, are better equipped to take the lead and initiate touching. Do it whenever you can, using simple gestures such as to touch your bipolar's hand, gently caress a shoulder, and other such contacts.

Of course, kissing and making love rate higher and should not be avoided. Set a romantic mood or simply light a candle, but do not pass on the opportunity for a night of lovemaking. This extra-special bonding will help both of you get past the difficult times more easily and give you the strength to survive the depths of depression or the highs of mania. A relationship built on touching and focused on creating a strong bond can use touching and kissing to help break the disorder's hold on your bipolar and become a way for your bipolar to break these holds themselves. There is no doubt, either clinically or practically, that bonding and reconnecting are absolutely essential if your unique, loving relationship is to survive.

This brings up the subject of sex. If your partner is on an SSRI (Zoloft, Celexia, Effexor, etc.), you need to be aware that these drugs can cause sexual side effects. The most common is "prolonged inability to reach orgasm." The joke in our support group is, "Yeah, about four days long!" This is a real problem, and you need to talk to your doctor about it. As one man said, "I was already depressed, the last thing I needed to do was give up sex or have problems in bed." There are many antidepressants on the market today, so if one is not right for you, see your doctor and ask for changes or consider adding Viagra or one of the other new erectile dysfunction drugs currently on the market (Cialis and Levitra are the newest at this writing).

Men also need to have their testosterone levels checked. A simple blood test will provide the answer, and low testosterone will not only explain erectile dysfunction, but it can also be a fundamental cause of depression. Last but not least, there are manual penis pumps, penis implants, and shots.

Always be well informed and know your options. Sex is not everything, but it is a vital life function and shouldn't be sacrificed without a fight. If you and your partner are not ready to give it up, don't. Seek out ways in which you can overcome the challenges.

Dating

Get Out—even if it's only for lunch somewhere. Just the two of you, time alone, time together—a chance to reconnect. Mark and I try and get away for weekends as often as possible, staying in clean, inexpensive motels or small Bed and Breakfast lodgings. These two or three days of relaxation and diversion help us focus on ourselves and each other, both as individuals and as a couple.

Lack of communication is a killer, but lack of intimacy and the feeling of "closeness" are perhaps even worse. Get back to holding hands, having quiet conversations, enjoying laughter and play whenever you can. Be mindful of your moments together and aware of the feelings you experience. Dating is critical to the survival of a bipolar marriage.

These are some of the excuses for not dating and reconnecting: "I'm too angry, too tired, too emotionally drained, too afraid to feel happy again just to be let down." Reconnecting with your partner is something that you have to want more than anything else, more than you want your hurt, your pain or even your disappointment.

"But," you say, "I've tried, I'm too tired to try again." My reply is that *you have then made a decision*, conscious or not. But remember, you have the right to change your mind, to make a new choice, and if you and your partner choose to go forward with a commitment to your relationship, go forward FULL STEAM AHEAD, hold nothing back, make no excuses, give it 100% of yourself.

You may have to start small because unbridled commitment is difficult, at best. But start!

Don't make this too complicated. Go to a movie or just take a walk. The important thing is that the two of you reconnect often and continually, through words and actions, to reconfirm your love for each other. Trust us, a history of dating will make it easier to cope when the next mood swing comes along.

How often to "date?" Try to do something together at least once a week—a movie, lunch, a picnic in the park—and try to get away once a month, even if it's just for a brief, overnight trip.

I love you

*"Even on my worst days
and in my deepest depressions,
I love Debra and she loves me."*
Mark Meehl

According to Mark, this is true even on the days when (as he has actually said) "I hate her and the ground she walks on!" Thank goodness, doesn't happen as often these days as it has in the past. "This knowledge keeps her sane," Mark says, "and it keeps me grounded; it keeps both of us committed to our relationship. It also helps Debra survive the chaos of living with a bipolar—me."

Because of their unique chemical imbalances, bipolars often wax and wane in their feelings of emotional love, so you must reinforce the idea of "Intellectual Love." Take comfort in knowing that it exists, that you have it, and that you can both learn to exult in those moments when you and your bipolar can feel

"Emotional Love." In the midst of chaos, love is always your lifeline, and you will discover comfort and confidence in the fact that you "love" each other.

Our therapist introduced us to this idea the first time the subject of love came up in our therapy, at a moment when Mark was very depressed. As a woman, I had always thought that love was supposed to be warm and fuzzy, because even when I'm mad at Mark I can still feel the love for him in my heart, and that never changes. So, a few months later, as the two of us were walking on the beach after a particularly chaotic afternoon for Mark, I asked him if he wanted to hold my hand as we walked together. He took my hand but then looked at me and said, "Even if I do not show you at the time, I always love you intellectually, and I know that the *feelings* will return soon. My knowing that keeps me connected to you."

It is important that you learn to say "I Love You" to each other—*out loud!* I understand that it can be very painful and overwhelmingly difficult to say at times when your bipolar is in the midst of an up or down cycle, but these three words really do have the power to break through rage, manic behavior and depression. They can bring comfort and reassurance to the bipolar, and as I have noticed over and over, voicing the sentiment can help me to *depersonalize the words and actions resulting from Mark's cycling.*

By staying focused on your love you are each better able to reduce the impact and importance of otherwise painful words or deeds.

"I Love You" can also become a powerful affirmation. If you have not said these words to your partner recently, try doing it—even better, do it three times a day. Again, you do not have to "feel" it at the time; it's a behavior choice, but it will make an enormous emotional difference to both of you.

Attend a retreat

Take time to recharge yourself and refocus your relationship. Retreats offer an opportunity to become immersed in a calm, peaceful, relaxing environment. If, as a non-bipolar partner, you can attend one for families or partners of bipolars, all the better, because you will interact with people who truly understand and share your experiences. Retreats enable you to focus in a wholistic way on your mental, spiritual and emotional well-being. Retreats also provide a safe, neutral environment in which valuable techniques for reconnecting, recharging and recommitting to progress are built into the agenda. What more appropriate environment could you create for reaffirming your love and commitment?

If you should attend a retreat for married couples, find out whether the facilitator is experienced with mental health issues

If you are absolutely unable to attend a retreat, get away for a long weekend without kids, friends or family and only as close to any other living human being as you need to be in order to survive.

Other Practical Matters

Two documents
you must have . . .
even if you are married

If it is necessary to commit the bipolar in your life to a hospital, this document—a **Mental/Medical Power of Attorney (POA)**—will allow you to remain in control of the process and involved in the treatment and medication decisions that are made.

A Mental/Medical Power of Attorney may vary somewhat from state to state, but state-specific versions for most states can be found on the internet. Specifically, we recommend using your state's website to look for a FREE copy of the necessary form and to obtain the regulations associated with a proper Mental/Medical POA. Generally, you can find a printable copy of your state's POA online on the page relating to the Attorney General's office, which is the office that handles such forms.

In some states, even if you are married to or the parent of a bipolar, you may not be able to have your bipolar committed without his or her expressed permission—thus the need for this form. And, very importantly, without this form you may also find yourself unable to influence those vital medication and treatment decisions.

Legislation and regulation can be paradoxical at best, so be careful to read everything very carefully as you prepare a POA. In our state (Arizona), for example, a bipolar may individually refuse to be admitted or medicated, which makes absolutely no sense at all because in the midst of mania or depression, a bipolar is no more able to make sound decisions regarding their health and treatment than to fly to the moon. Yet the state legislature has decided that bipolars somehow need to be given this control over their treatment. Brilliant! A Power of Attorney, correctly written and properly signed, though, can trump the state law. Therefore, in order to prevent your empowered and possibly delusional bipolar from arbitrarily refusing help or treatment, be sure to execute a Medical/Mental POA so that you can exercise rational control over the process should that ever become necessary. This kind of POA can be likened to having a life jacket when your ship is sinking. It's also a bit like having an insurance policy—you don't *want* to need it, but if an accident occurs, you are sure glad you had it!

Mark and I have a plan and a Mental/Medical POA. We put ours together when he was well so that in a time of crisis we would have it. Luckily, we have not needed it—and we don't plan on needing it—but . . .

We recommend that you have several copies of this form signed and notarized.

Keep one in each of your cars and one in your files at home. If you are traveling or away from home, the one in your car will help you deal with any emergency, regardless of the state you are in at the time. The one at home insures that if one copy is lost you will always have a backup should you need one. The second document that you must have available and properly executed is a **Medical Release of Information (MRI)**. *This is an absolute necessity if you want any doctor, hospital or therapist to discuss medication, treatment plans or diagnosis with your partner.* Under the current laws (HIPPA) you, as a spouse or partner, are not entitled to any of this information without this form. You also need to sign a copy for your doctors and therapist so they can talk to one another about you. Again, if your therapist thinks that your medication needs to be changed, he or she needs permission to contact your doctor on your behalf and discuss your behavior or treatment. The MRI is the document that can do that.

We can't emphasize this enough—the major reason that patients are so often misdiagnosed or improperly medicated is that the treatment "team" members are not all on the same page. Also, remember that the therapist spends an hour a week with you, while most prescribing physicians spend only 15 minutes with you, often after weeks of no contact. So it stands to reason that the therapist may actually be ahead of the doctor in spotting a significant change that needs to be addressed *with medication.*

Since the basic language of a Mental/Medical Power of Attorney is generally standardized, you can type this form yourself. An example may be found in appendix 5 at the back of this book or on the Meehl Foundation website.

Get a letter

Get a letter of diagnosis from your therapist and doctor. Bipolars have a tendency to get in trouble with the law, and the families of bipolars occasionally need police intervention. We hear many stories of problems with the law or of the need to have an out-of-control bipolar partner arrested for his or her own protection. Within each of these stories we hear either how the intervention of the police has gone well or how it has gone terribly wrong. Based on these diverse and opposing conversations, here is what we know: you must be able to show the police that they are clearly dealing with a person who has Bipolar Disorder. This gives you the leverage to insist that the bipolar be *properly treated and medicated while in their jurisdiction.* Be sure always to *get the name and badge number of the police officers involved in any situation with a bipolar.* Like anything in life, if they know that you know their names, the police tend to behave better.

I am reminded of a story about a therapist with an adult son who was to fly with him and his wife to their home. To start with, the son was late arriving at the airport and was the last to board the flight. Walking to the plane, the wife, turning to her husband, said, "Oh, my! What are we going to do?" You see, even from a distance she could tell that her son was manic just by the way he was walking. Of course, as the son started to board the plane there was a problem and he was arrested, removed from the plane and taken to jail. As soon as the plane carrying the parents arrived at its destination airport, the father phoned the police to inform them that his son was bipolar and was obviously manic and sick. The policeman told him that they could "handle anything." The father took names and numbers anyway and told the police that should anything happen to his son while he was in their custody they should expect to be sued to the full extent and letter of the law and that he had several personal friends who were lawyers.

As the night wore on, the son's condition deteriorated further until he was tearing up the cell and hanging from the bars. The police finally called the father in the middle of the night to find out what to do and to make arrangements to release the son into the father's custody, which they did the next morning, dropping all the charges.

Should you need an attorney, that advocate must clearly understand that the client is bipolar. It really helps if the lawyer is experienced in representing mentally ill clients.

No matter how trivial or serious the legal situation, getting treatment is the goal throughout the process. In the event of a conviction and sentencing, ask to talk to the judge and present the letter. Jail time versus hospitalization isn't a hard decision to make. With proper documentation, you will have a better chance on appeal that the judge will agree to hospitalization over incarceration.

Know the admissions policy

In the event that you need to have your bipolar partner treated at the hospital against his or her will, you must know the answers to the following questions:

- ◆ What is the admissions policy for your local mental hospital?
- ◆ Where is the hospital located?
- ◆ For how long can you have someone committed for evaluation?
- ◆ What is the treatment protocol?

- What paperwork do you need to have in hand at the time of commitment?
- Will the authorities contact your primary therapist or doctor?

And, by all means, visit the facility in your area that you might need to use. Do not wait until a crisis arises, only to discover that the local facility is a low-budget hole-in-the-wall staffed with poorly trained doctors and clinicians. Should you need to call 911, you have the right to request, when the police or ambulance shows up, that the patient be taken a specific facility.

Many of these questions can be answered over the phone and your answers should be decided before you need them. Do not forget to have a Medical/Mental Power of Attorney and the Release of Medical Information paperwork with you.

My doctor won't go to the hospital

This is a situation in which a Medical/Mental Power of Attorney document is a critical.

Most medication doctors do not go to the mental health hospitals when your bipolar is hospitalized. This doesn't mean that they won't communicate with the hospital and the attending doctors there. However, it is advisable that you provide the hospital with your prescribing doctor's name and phone number, plus a list of the medications the bipolar is currently taking. Hospitals will generally discuss changes in medications and dosages with your doctor and send copies of their records after release. If you should find that the hospital and doctor are not communicating, the POA or the MRI will help you facilitate their communication.

If possible, find out how long the hospital expects to keep your bipolar, then make an appointment with your regular doctor for a day or two after the projected release date. If the date of release should change, you can always reschedule, but scheduling ahead is better than waiting a week or longer, which is what will happen if you wait until the release date.

Three business cards

There are three business cards you should always have available:

- your therapist's card,
- your medication doctor's card, and
- your personal card.

Don't have a personal card? Make one and be sure it contains all of the information necessary to allow people to contact you. If you don't have such a card—or if you'd rather not have one made up—your regular business card will probably be more than sufficient. You may need a personal card for the police, though, and for many of the people you encounter in social service.

Beware of Trojan horses

Know which of your friends and family members are positive, uplifting, supportive and caring influences—and which of them are not.

Mental illness is very difficult for "normal" people to accept. Look how hard it was for you and your bipolar to accept the diagnosis when it became "real" for you.

Out of concern and in an effort to be supportive, friends, neighbors—and even some family members—may possibly respond with a range of negative emotions, which could cause chaos in your life as a result of their meddling. If necessary, be willing to limit the amount and kind of contact you have with them. Be willing to be clear about what input and actions are acceptable. Identify boundaries and be completely open and honest in your communication. Be aware that family will have a number of things that they want you to try, such as anger management classes, motivational coaching, green tea and just "pulling yourself together and up by your bootstraps." There may be prayer, fasting and symbolic bloodlettings, too. Getting used to this new idea about someone they thought they knew well may be very difficult for some, particularly if they don't truly understand that Bipolar Disorder is a chemical imbalance in the brain, and that its victims have no more control over that fact than the diabetic has over having diabetes.

Families are usually more comfortable using terms like eccentric, strange, lazy, or weird rather than the more hard-edged, frightening terms "bipolar" or "mentally ill."

Here are some of the disorders so far known to be caused by chemical imbalances in the brain and currently thought to be genetic:

- Generalized anxiety disorder (GAD), displayed by people who worry incessantly about money, family, work or health, to the point of high anxiety. GAD affects about four million people.

- Obsessive-compulsive disorders (OCD), suffered by individuals who are compelled to conduct repetitive rituals such as hoarding, checking, arranging, hand washing or counting. A classic OCD example is an 80-year-old woman with 50 cats or a child who cannot go to sleep because his shoes are not lined up correctly.

- Specific Phobias affect about 6.3 million people and are described by intense fear of something that is really not a threat. Phobias also have no rhyme or reason, as you may be able to rappel down a cliff but cannot tolerate a ride in a five-story elevator.

Today, chemical dependency in a family is not considered out of the ordinary, and goodness knows, it is far better than the seemingly ugly label of "mental illness." However, the fact is that many families will go to great lengths to see chemical abuse or just plain laziness as the core issue when, in fact, the real issue is mental illness.

To avoid Trojan Horses (hurtful actions represented as being helpful), be honest. Let people know about the illness. Discuss how it manifests itself. Let people know that Bipolar Disorder is not contagious even though it is a genetic disorder.

Family members who are informed to the level of their comfort can then learn more easily to be more supportive and encouraging to affected family members instead of labeling and blaming them. Through observation and awareness you will be able to recognize Trojan Horses and thus be better able to diminish the impact they have on your life.

When family members are ready, they will count the number of "weird" family members, the number of suicides, and the number of depressed (they might call them "lazy") family members on their own, so you will not have to do it for them. Until they are ready to accept the truths about Bipolar Disorder, you may have to hold them at arm's length.

Who's the fallback?

If something should happen to you, who will take care of the bipolar in your family? This serious issue needs to be addressed and revisited again and again over time. In a year or five or ten, the person you think is right for the job today may no longer be right. Think carefully and consider all of the possible options, from assisted living to a family member or a friend.

Hiring a personal assistant for two hours a day may be all that you need during this time. But whatever is right for your family, you must have a plan and have it detailed in clearly written instructions.

I know an engineer who functions quite well at work but is unable to shop for groceries, balance her checkbook, or cook a meal. This is not a question of intelligence or laziness. She simply cannot function in these areas, so she has hired an assistant to do certain things for her. The assistant also feeds her dogs, and is even charged with paying the rent and utilities when this bipolar engineer is sick and in the hospital. Remember, no one automatically tells the landlord or the utility companies, credit card companies, etc. what is going on, so unless you have someone appointed by Power of Attorney to sign the checks, it doesn't get done.

Since most bipolars are continuously anxious about the future, the thought of your dying can cause great anxiety and should be discussed before there is a crisis. The questions to ask are:

♦ Which family member or friend do you want to help you first?

♦ How long do they need to stay?

♦ Do you need help in picking an assistant?

♦ Will you need to live with a family member or friend for a while?

♦ And finally, do you want your partner, in a time of crisis, to have to decide to cremate you or bury you or to determine where to put your remains? Get a properly executed will (consult an attorney)

Again, there are many vital decisions to be made in every crisis situation, and waiting until the last minute serves no one.

Americans with Disabilities Act (ADA)

Take the time to read and understand YOUR rights. It will make life much easier for you and your bipolar. Both of you have rights and you should know them.

This is a multifaceted Act that affects a number of areas of your life, from employment and education to health care and housing. We encourage you to spend some time on the ADA website's home page, which you will find online at www.usdoj.gov/crt/ada/ada, and from there you can go to the various links that most directly address your concerns.

Mental illness is covered in employment, under the regulations of the Equal Employment Opportunities Commission (EEOC), for such things as job restructuring, modified work schedules and reassignment. As an example, employers may not ask about the existence, nature or severity of a disability, but they may ask about a candidate's ability to do the job.

The ADA deals with education issues through the Department of Education. In light of the No Child Left Behind Act, it is important that you understand how your local and state governments are dealing with students with a mental illness. Under the ADA, the student has the right to specialized training and programs designed to make the education process easier. With an Individualized Education Plan (IEP) in place, accommodations can be made to help with testing and issues relating to behavior and the individual needs of the student.

Throughout local, state and federal government offices and programs, this Act serves to insure that bipolars and others suffering from mental illness are protected and accommodated as they attempt to live a normal life.

Meet with the school

What happens when your child is manic and raging at school?

Let school officials know about your child's condition, and be sure also that security personnel at school realize that your child may behave in certain ways at certain times and that such behavior may well be a part of their illness.

Ask what school officials know and understand about manic or depressed children.

Who is your primary contact at the school? If there is no one person who will act as your contact, be sure that the school gives you the names and a phone numbers of several responsible adults— teachers, counselors, assistant principals, etc.—folks who can resolve issues with your children and assist you in establishing reasonable criteria for responsibility.

Be sure to meet with the school nurse and leave a printed set of instructions for any medications. Include your name and phone numbers on that list, as well as those of your child's therapist and prescribing doctor. By the way, it is a wise idea to ask the nurse to sign for the list so you will have proof of responsibly informing a school official about how to treat your child and what to do in the event of an emergency.

When dealing with schools you cannot afford to be meek. You need to be sure that those in whose care you leave your child understand Bipolar Disorder—what it is, how it displays itself, and what you expect of them in terms of your child's treatment.

Let's face it, at one time or another your child will be out of control, and unless you have prepared the school to handle this situation, the outcome of an episode can be disastrous for everyone—the school, you, and—most importantly—your child.

At the same time, your child must be clear on the rules of behavior that he or she is expected to follow when in the school environment. Teach your child to communicate with teachers and counselors, letting them know immediately when a manic or depressive episode seems to be coming on. Teach your child how to recognize and mindfully respond to feelings and emotions and how to communicate effectively, without fear, with school officials.

Tell the teachers

Bipolar Disorder is a disability and is covered under the Americans with Disabilities Act (ADA). If you are raising a bipolar student, meet with the child's teachers, provide them with an information sheet on Bipolar Disorder, and ask for accommodations and an IEP

(Instructional Education Plan) that assists a child who has any kind of disability. For instance, if your child had a hearing loss, he or she would need to sit up front in class, or if a child has dyslexia, that child would need extra time for taking tests. Awareness has been heightened recently by legislation. There are *many* accommodations for many kinds of disabilities. These accommodations will aid your student. Teachers should be asked to make allowances for tests that are scheduled at times when your child is in a manic or depressed period by permitting your student to make up the test later, when balance has been restored. The same should hold true for homework.

Create a team atmosphere and school will go better for your student. Is this a lot of work? Yeah! Do you do any work that is more important than your child?

Last but not least, if your child is not thriving at school, make changes. Consider your alternatives.

- Can you or a friend or a relative home school the child?
- How about attending a charter school with flexible hours? Yes, some schools do not start at 8 a.m.—some start later or earlier.
- Some schools specialize in the arts, even at the grade school level.

◆ Have you considered a private school? "No money," you say? There is usually a list of anonymous sponsors who will pay for your child's education. You need only to ask at the school you select.

Remember that most of our schools are designed to educate the median population, the average student. Most schools are not equipped to handle the very gifted, who may have disabilities. For instance, Charles Schwab, today the head of a major stock brokerage firm, failed miserably all through school, and Albert Einstein failed the first four grades.

There are many ways of learning, and the trick is to find the way that works for your child and sets him or her on a course for success and not for failure.

Final
Thoughts

Borderline
Personality Disorder

The following section on Borderline Personality Disorder (BPD) was written for us by Carol Dagenet, M.Ed., Social Services Director of the East Mesa (AZ) Healthcare Center, who has worked for many years with BPD patients, as well as with their families alongside treating professionals in both psychology and medicine.

A personality disorder is a rather unique animal. According to Gregory W. Lester, Ph.D., a "normal" personality is defined as *"the ability to access sufficiently diverse traits, tools and strategies to adapt to the changing, differing demands and goals of one's life."* A personality disorder would then be *"a disorder in the way a person deals with the demands and circumstances in life."*

You can be fairly confident that you are in the company of someone with a personality disorder if, when the person leaves, you feel rotten. Such a person is accustomed to relieving emotional pain by transferring the feeling to you. Another telltale sign is that, despite all the tears and sadness you may hear, you simply cannot muster any compassion for him or her.

Personality disorders often exist in combination with other mental health issues, and it can be difficult to differentiate Borderline Personality

Disorder from Bipolar Disorder, as Bipolar Disorder has similar symptoms. The greatest difficulty with Borderline Personality Disorder (or any other personality disorder, for that matter) is that the symptoms often do not respond to medication as well as do those of better-known psychiatric illnesses such as Schizophrenia, Anxiety, Bipolar Disorder and Depression. A personality disorder is unlike Bipolar Disorder in that it is not caused by a chemical imbalance in the brain. It is a *missing function* in the personality. With any personality disorder, those who suffer from it lack the ability to see their part of a problem. Insight is an unfamiliar tool to use for problem solving. Looking at one's self objectively simply is not possible for them because it is not in their repertoire of coping skills.

Neurologists first used the phrase "Borderline Personality" in the 1800s to describe a subset of neurotic patients who didn't get better with therapy. These patients were not psychotic (out of touch with reality), nor were they really neurotic; they were on the "borderline". This is still the term-of-art used in psychiatry. *Tabor's Medical Cyclopedia 19* defines Borderline Personality as: *"A personality disorder in which there is difficulty in maintaining stable interpersonal relationships and self-image. This manifests itself as unpredictable and impulsive behavior, outbursts of anger, irritability, sadness, and fear. Self-mutilation or suicidal behavior may be present. Sometimes there is a chronic feeling of emptiness or boredom."* Additionally, consider that in the person with Borderline Personality Disorder the sense of self is context-dependent.

A professional in the field describes patients with Borderline Personality Disorder as "people who have trouble with borders or boundaries."

Effective treatment of Borderline Personality Disorder includes lots of boundary setting, which gives the patient the experiences required to learn new skills and behaviors.

Dialectical Behavior Therapy (DBT), which we discussed on page 60, has proven successful in working with these people.

The goal of therapeutic counseling in this situation is to instill the missing functions. This can take five to seven years with a good therapist who is experienced with treating Borderline Personality Disorder.

For those of you who frequently interact with a person who suffers from a Borderline Personality Disorder, watch for that person to attempt to get you to rescue him or her or to get you to agree that he or she is being mistreated. At this point, beware! As soon as you "rescue" or "agree," somehow you become the "bad guy." A perceived loss of love can trigger a person with Borderline Personality Disorder to become very manipulative and volatile. Sometimes all you can do is respond with empathy. "Gee, it must feel really bad to have your boyfriend not talk to you while he is studying for finals." Never mind that the boyfriend has to take his medical boards in the morning for his M.D.! The Borderline has little ability to deal with this kind of situation, as it is fraught with abandonment issues.

Consider alternatives

Returning now to Bipolar Disorder and remembering from earlier reading that there can be only a few absolutes in the life of a bipolar, you must be willing to consider alternatives.

By considering all of the possible alternatives, you will become open to change, receptive to the learning process you will need to participate in, and able develop new pathways for yourself.

When Mark and I are confronted with problems or are considering new ideas, we try to look at the issues from as many angles as possible until together we find a solution that will work in the moment and, insofar as possible, for both of us. By simply being open to the possibilities, we have often discovered that the solution we settle on in any given situation arises from an alternative we wouldn't (or couldn't) have considered at all a couple of years ago.

As we have learned more about Bipolar Disorder itself and have lived through all of its ups and downs, our willingness to consider alternatives has consistently broadened. The new doors that have opened have brought forth new opportunities that, in turn, have made living with Bipolar Disorder much easier for both of us.

By remaining open to alternatives, we have also become better able to adjust our thoughts and behaviors as we deal with triggers. In therapy, open-mindedness has allowed us to be more receptive to alternative interpretations of past and current events and more acutely aware of their impact on our current and future life together.

As we define and redefine the absolutes in our life, we have seen our life's direction change (sometimes radically), our understanding increase, and our relationship blossom as never before.

Alternative supplements and treatments

What is important to remember here is that just because something is "natural" does not mean that it is right or safe for you. Plutonium is natural, but I would not recommend drinking it. Always check with your doctor before embarking on any radical, new course of medication or diet supplementation.

St. Johns Wort is prescribed in some European countries for mild or moderate depression. Studies have shown that although it may be effective for some people in some cases of very mild to moderate depression, it has little or no effect on severe depression. It is not a prescription drug in the U.S. but can be found in most health food stores.

SAM-e (S-adenosyl-L-Methionine) is a naturally occurring and essential substance in the body and plays an important role in regulating the brain's dopamine and serotonin. Studies on the effectiveness or SAM-e show it to be more effective than sugar pills in relieving depressive symptoms, but when compared to prescription medications commonly used to treat depression, SAM-e yielded no better results. In another study, patients with major depression who were taking antidepressant added SAM-e to their diets. Half of them showed measurable improvement, and nearly half went into remission and were no longer experiencing symptoms when the study ended.

Omega-3 fatty acids are found in highest concentrations in salmon and tuna. The American Heart Association recommends two servings a week of these fish (four ounces of salmon or six ounces of tuna) for heart health. New research also suggests that one to four grams (1000mg-4000mg) of Omega-3 fatty acids may be needed for good brain function and to help with slowing the onset of some symptoms of Alzheimer's disease.

Transcranial Magnetic Stimulation (TMS) is under investigation for the treatment of depression. The therapy is delivered via a hand-held device that generates magnetic bursts of energy when it is placed against the scalp. Treatments do not require surgery, hospitalization or anesthesia, and there is no pain associated with the treatment. Sessions usually take 30 minutes and are recommended five days a week for 4-5 weeks to be effective. As with any procedure there is risk. Though extremely rare, seizures have been reported.

Vagus Nerve Stimulation involves the implantation of a device similar to a pacemaker, which is programmed to deliver a small electrical impulse to the brain. It has been approved by the FDA for seizures but is not currently approved for use in the treatment of depression.

Magnetic Stimulation Therapy (MST) is one of the newest procedures on the frontier. MST produces a seizure and requires anesthesia. The benefits at this time appear to be that it can target specific portions of the brain and that it does not affect the memory or concentration of the patient.

Electric Shock Therapy (ECT) is still the Gold Standard for depression that is not improved through medication. Unlike the movie O*ne Flew Over The Cuckoo's Nest, starring* Jack Nicholson, in which he was a mentally ill patient who was receiving ECT with out anesthesia, ECT has come a long way. The treatment requires anesthesia and a hospital stay, but is it very humane. It may, however, have a negative effect on memory. In some cases there has been a loss of memory of up to three months on both sides of the treatment. Usually most patients say that is was well worth it, though, to have their lives back.

Finally, for the attorney, we do not endorse or recommend the use of any specific treatment or medication. Our purpose is to educate you on the possibilities. Both your physician and your therapist should first approve any specific treatment and all medications or supplements.

Exercise and eat right

Inactivity can contribute significantly to depression as well as to diminished health. Both of you—the bipolar and the partner—need to exercise. The physical benefits of exercise are, of course, well documented.

This doesn't mean that you have to join a gym. For sit-ups, push-ups and chin-ups there really isn't a lot you need. Walking together can provide both great exercise and some private time together. Whatever you do, you need to exercise.

For the bipolar, exercise will be an important part of the constant effort to minimize weight gain caused by some medications. The most important benefit for both of you is the ability of exercise to help you from slipping into depression yourself or helping you get out of depression.

In addition to exercise, eating right is critical for the bipolar. Skipping meals such as breakfast only lead to a sugar low, which then leads to over eating and subsequent swings in blood sugar, causing abnormal storage of fat. Eating a low carbohydrate diet can help, and cutting back on the sugar consumption is a must. Snacks at our house look like fresh vegetables, (not fruit) nuts, whole grains, eggs, cheese, low carbohydrate yogurt, and cottage cheese. Mark has an eight-hour fasting blood sugar test about every two months, as he currently is taking Zyprexa, which can produce a form of insulin-dependent diabetes, as do a number of anti-psychotic medications currently in use. So far, we have not had any problems, but Mark no longer buys Snickers by the bagful.

Marijuana

This subject will cause difficulty for some readers, but it needs to be addressed. We realize that there are moral (and some significant legal) considerations that you will need to deal with, but . . .

. . . there is more than enough anecdotal evidence of marijuana's significant ability to help treat Bipolar Disorder, particularly regarding the treatment of mania and depression in many people.[4]

If you are using marijuana to help with this illness, let your doctor and therapist know. They may need to take that fact into consideration when making their medication decisions or as they decide how to handle manic and depressive episodes.

A caution: Research clearly shows that marijuana is NOT an option for children and teenagers. Until approximately the age of 21, the brain is still developing, and it is thought that marijuana can interfere with brain development

As a practical matter, we do not believe that most people benefit from any narcotics or stimulants, so we highly caution against their use in any circumstance. Bipolar Disorder is a serious illness caused by an imbalance of certain chemicals in the brain; to

---

[4] (See: The use of cannabis as a mood stabilizer in Bipolar Disorder: anecdotal evidence and the need for clinical research, by Grinspoon, L; Bakalar, JB. Department of Psychiatry, Harvard Medical School, Boston, MA. Journal of Psychoactive Drugs 1998, Apr-Jun; 30(2):171-7)

introduce powerful stimulants (like cocaine or methamphetamines) that are known to damage the brain can trigger Bipolar Disorder and should *never* be allowed or tolerated. If you are faced with a drug problem, let your doctor know and begin a treatment and recovery program as soon as possible.

Please do not use this section as an excuse to go through life stoned to the bone. We believe in marijuana for its medical and medicinal purposes, not for its recreational potential, if any.

Suicide is not an option

Self-destruction is an absolutely permanent state of affairs, but it's **not** a solution. Whatever else you do or don't do, make a commitment, set boundaries, and *agree on the principle that suicide is not an option for your bipolar.*

The bipolar condition isn't one that anyone chooses, and once it is present, even when not properly diagnosed, many days and nights are really difficult, confusing, frustrating, and angering to rage. But none of that—no matter how bad—is an excuse for suicide.

Once diagnosed, every bipolar should understand that thoughts of suicide are a dire warning that medications need to be changed or adjusted and that whatever has triggered the depression leading to suicidal thoughts needs to be identified and dealt with.

Successful suicide is always devastating for the families and friends who are left behind. The act itself ends the pain, but it leaves much more pain behind—for everyone who remains alive. Even in the depths of depression, you cannot justify that the world (your world) will be better if you die, regardless of what your mind is telling you.

As partner to a bipolar, here are some of the questions to ask your partner about his or her thoughts of suicide:

◆ Do you feel safe or do you have the need to hurt yourself?

◆ Have you made a plan to take you life?

◆ How long have you been thinking about this?

These are important questions and *must* be asked! Rest assured, you are not going to give your partner any "new ideas." Every bipolar has had *thoughts* about suicide, but most decide that they don't have a need, a want or a cause to do it. **If your bipolar partner has a lethal plan and the means whereby to implement it—and feels that there is no other option—this is an emergency and you need to call the crisis team and/or the police for assistance. The bipolar needs to be hospitalized. Do not take *no* for an answer!**

Will it get worse?

Absolutely! Un-medicated and with no therapy, Bipolar Disorder will definitely get worse. It will become a nightmare. Medicated and not in therapy? Yes, it will still get worse—you will have the same old behaviors, just not as frequently. Remember that part of this illness is environmental and depends upon how you and your bipolar handle triggers.

Untreated or medicated, the bipolar will continue to repeat certain patterns of destructive responses to triggers and may seek to self-medicate through alcohol and substance abuse. These, of course, will only make the chemical imbalance—and the brain's reactions and patterning to triggers—much worse.

As the illness progresses, the bipolar will begin to see and hear things, particularly when exhausted. Eventually, the patient will become delusional and even suicidal. At the same time, other illnesses affecting the bipolar will continue to impact upon behaviors and belief systems.

Remember that with bipolars there is a 99% chance that there will be another illness or addiction to deal with, and that, too, will most likely remain untreated and un-medicated.

The reactions and behaviors described in the DSM Criteria listed in the back of this book will continue to heighten, becoming more and more severe as the bipolar increasingly loses control of emotions and swings from one mood to the next, up and down, from emotion to reaction to emotion to reaction. When this cycle is prevalent, neither you nor your bipolar can expect even a smidgen of normalcy in your life, and that will continue for as long as the bipolar remains un-medicated and not in therapy with a qualified professional.

However, it has been conclusively demonstrated that with medication and therapy there can be stability or remission of symptoms, and at times you can both enjoy a "return to normalcy."

The first step is to get medication—*and to get it right*. As I have pointed out previously, this process is not always smooth and easy and can take months to achieve. Until the doctor determines the right medications and establishes the proper dosages, you and your "lab rat"— as Mark has called himself—will have to depend on therapy and personal mindfulness to get through the rough spots and cope with the adjustments. However, even during this period, both of you can begin to get control of the illness and reduce its negative effects on your life together by using behavioral therapy, medication, and an honest commitment to mindfulness, growth and change management. In this scenario, it will get better.

Finally, for life to get *really* better, you must take care of *yourself*. In fact, physically and psychologically, you must take care of yourself *first*. If you are to live with the bipolar in this world and also "get better," you should have a therapist, a support group/person, and sometimes medication for yourself. Just as the bipolar needs a team, so do you. Build it and rely on it to help you take care of yourself.

We believe that through the technique of **mindfulness**, coupled with emotional stability and spiritual well-being, as well as via compliance with medication instructions and ongoing therapy (for each and both of you, as indicated), you, too, can have a fulfilling and loving relationship with the bipolar in your life, and you can and should expect to lead an enriching and rewarding life—together.

Appendices

1. Recommended Reading

Here are a few of the books we have read and found to be helpful. Not all of them deal with Bipolar Disorder; they instead deal with such topics as mindfulness, healing and personal growth. In all of them you will find information and comfort to use in your daily life. As we have stressed throughout this book, recovery and healing lie in knowledge.

The four books you must read immediately

The Four Agreements, Don Miguel Ruiz. Amber-Allen, 1997

The Seven Spiritual Laws of Success, Deepak Chopra. Amber-Allen, 1994

Stop Walking on Eggshells, Paul T. Mason & Randi Kreger. New Harbinger Publications, Oakland, CA, 1998

Codependent's Guide to the Twelve Steps, Melody Beattie. Fireside/Parkside, New York, 1990

Bipolar Disorder and Depression

The Bipolar Disorder Survival Guide, David J. Miklowitz, Ph.D. The Guilford Press, New York, 2002

Depression Fallout: The Impact of Depression on Couples and What You Can Do to Preserve the Bond. Anne Sheffield, Harper Collins, New York, 2003

Depressed & Anxious: The Dialectical Behavior Therapy Workbook, Thomas Marra, Ph.D. New Harbinger, Oakland, CA, 2004

BP magazine—monthly publication - P.O. Box 59, Buffalo, NY 14205-0059
This is a wonderful magazine and a "must" subscription for anyone dealing with this illness. The cost of a one-year subscription is only $19.95 for four issues.

Mindfulness and personal growth

The Bible, Torah, Koran, etc.,

Living Buddha, Living Christ, Thich Nhat Hanh. Riverhead Books, New York, 1995

What You Think Of Me Is None of My Business, Terry Cole-Whittaker. Oak Tree Publications, San Diego, 1979

Beyond Codependency: and getting better all the time, Melody Beattie. Harper/Hazelden, New York, 1989

You Can Heal Your Life, Louise L. Hay. Hay House, San Diego, CA, 1999

The Power is Within You, Louise L. Hay. Hay House, San Diego, CA, 1991

Borderline Personality Disorder

I Hate You—Don't Leave Me: Understanding The Borderline Personality, Jerold J. Kreisman, MD, & Hal Straus. Avon Books, New York, 1989

2. Web Page Links

These are the sites we have found to be most useful to us in dealing with Mark's Bipolar Disorder and its impact on our family. There are thousands of sites on the Internet, so we have focused on quality, ease of maneuvering through the site and content that was helpful to the non-bipolar families and friends.

For information on a Medical Power of Attorney for your state, go to your state's attorney general's website

www.meehlfoundation.org
A website focused on the non-bipolar, providing information, resources and empowerment.

www.dbsalliance.org
Depression and Bipolar Support Alliance. A tremendous resource for any family dealing with the effects of depression and Bipolar Disorder.

www.webmd.com
Latest information on medications, side effects and use in treatment and therapy. Also a good source for a layman's explanation of Bipolar Disorder and medications, in addition to new trends in medication and treatment.

www.bphope.com
BPmagazine a new magazine filled with good information for bipolars and their families.

www.depression.org

www.nimh.nih.gov
National Institutes of Mental Health (NIMH). A must for anyone dealing with this illness.

www.nami.org
A support and advocacy organization of consumers, families, and friends of people with mental illness.

www.clarkhoward.com
One of the best sites available for consumer and financial information

www.ssa.gov
Social Security online.

www.va.gov
Veteran's Administration online.

www.yourwholenutrition.org

www.ods.od.nih.gov
National Institutes of Health Office of Dietary Supplements

www.nccam.nih.gov
National Center for Complimentary and Alternative Medicine

www.nlm.nih.gov
National Library of Medicine

www.amfoundation.org
Alternative Medicine Foundation

www.herbmed.org
HerbMed Database (Alternative Medicine Foundation)

www.allsupinc.com
Allsup provides help in filing for Social Security Benefits. They are fee based, but report a very high first time approval rate. They are worth the money.

3. Bipolar Disorder

Symptoms of mania (Highs): DSM-IV Criteria

- Increased physical and mental activity and energy.
- Heightened mood, exaggerated optimism and self-confidence
- Excessive irritability, aggressive behavior
- Decreased need for sleep without experiencing fatigue
- Grandiose delusion, inflated sense of self-importance
- Racing speech, racing thoughts, flight of ideas
- Impulsiveness, poor judgment, distractibility
- Reckless behavior
- In the most severe cases, delusions and hallucinations

Appears to the non-bipolar as...

- Irritable, angry or raging
- Racing thoughts, unable to concentrate, unable to hold a thought
- Fast talking, or talking incessantly
- Spending money like you were a millionaire
- Obsessive compulsive
- Grandiose ideas, wanting to start a horse farm and you have never owned a horse
- Positive thinking (Peter Pan thinking)
- Indiscriminate sexual encounters
- Wanting sex multiple times a day with a partner
- Aggressive, paranoid, psychotic, delusional (last stages)

Symptoms of depression (Lows): DSM-IV Criteria

- Prolonged sadness or unexplained crying spells
- Significant changes in appetite and sleep patterns
- Irritability, anger, worry, agitation, anxiety
- Pessimism, indifference
- Loss of energy, persistent lethargy
- Feelings of guilt, worthlessness
- Inability to take pleasure in former interests, social withdrawal
- Unexplained aches and pains
- Recurring thoughts of death or suicide

Appears to the non-bipolar as...

- Self-absorbed, unaware or unconcerned about the needs of others, demanding, selfish
- Manipulative
- Demeaning, critical of a partner or familiar friend
- Aloof, uncommunicative, unresponsive, withdrawn
- Combative, contrary, fractious, finding fault with everything, querulous
- Changeable and unpredictable; illogical and unreasonable
- Pleasant and charming in public, the opposite at home
- Uninterested in sex, dismissive or distrusting when a partner is tender or affectionate
- Increasingly dependent on alcohol and drugs, gambling, spending money
- Obsessively addicted to TV, computer games and online porn sites, subject to other compulsive distractions
- Likely to refer spontaneously to separation or divorce
- Prone to workaholism and avoidance of responsibility

4. Definitions from Tabor's Medical Dictionary

Borderline Personality Disorder. A personality disorder in which there is difficulty in maintaining stable interpersonal relationships and self-image. This manifests as unpredictable and impulsive behavior, outbursts of anger, irritability, sadness, and fear. Self-mutilation or suicidal behavior may be present. Sometimes there is a chronic feeling of emptiness or boredom.

Bipolar I Mood Disorder. A mood disorder characterized by the presence of only one manic episode and no past major depressive episodes that is not better accounted for by a psychotic disorder. The classes or specifiers of Bipolar I disorder include mild, moderate, severe without psychotic features, severe with psychotic features, in partial remission, in full remission, with catatonic features, and with postpartum onset.

Bipolar II Mood Disorder. A mood disorder characterized by the occurrence of one or more major depressive episodes, accompanied by at least one hypomanic episode. If manic or mixed episode mood disorders are present, the diagnosis of Bipolar I cannot be supported. Episodes of substance-induced mood disorder or a mood disorder due to drugs or toxin exposure preclude the diagnosis of Bipolar II mood disorder. In addition, the symptoms must cause clinically significant distress or impairment in social, occupational, or other important areas of functioning. The specifiers "hypomanic" or "depressed" are used to indicate the current or most recent episode.

Tabor's Nursing Diagnosis
(considerations)
Borderline Personality Disorder

Violence, risk for directed at self or others, Self-Mutilation: risk factors may include use of projection as a major defense mechanism, pervasive problems with negative transference, feelings of guilt/need to "punish" self, distorted sense of self, inability to cope with increased psychological or physiological tension in a healthy manner.

Anxiety [severe to panic] may be related to unconscious conflicts (experience of extreme stress), perceived threat to self-concept, unmet needs, possibly evidenced by easy frustration and feelings of hurt, abuse of alcohol/other drugs, transient psychotic symptoms and performance of self-mutilating acts.

Self-Esteem, chronic low identity, disturbed personal: may be related to lack of positive feedback, unmet dependency needs, retarded ego development/fixation at an earlier level of development, possibly evidenced by difficulty identifying self or defining self-boundaries, feelings of depersonalization, extreme mood changes, lack of tolerance of rejection or being alone, unhappiness with self, striking out at others, performance of ritualistic self-damaging acts, and belief that punishing self is necessary.

Social Isolation may be related to immature interests, unaccepted social behavior, inadequate personal resources, and inability to engage in satisfying personal relationships, possibly evidenced by alternating clinging and distancing behaviors, difficulty meeting expectations of others, experiencing feelings of difference from others, expressing interests inappropriate to developmental age, and exhibiting behavior unaccepted by dominant cultural group.

Bipolar Disorder

Violence, risk for, directed at others: risk factors may include irritability, impulsive behavior; delusional thinking; angry response when ideas are refuted or wishes denied; manic excitement, with possible indicators of threatening body language/verbalizations, increased motor activity, overt and aggressive acts; and hostility.

Nutrition: less than body requirements, imbalanced: may be related to inadequate intake in relation to metabolic expenditures, possibly evidenced by body weight 20% or more below ideal weight, observed inadequate intake, inattention to mealtimes, and distraction from task of eating; laboratory evidence of nutritional deficits/imbalances.

Poisoning, risk for lithium toxicity: risk factors may include narrow therapeutic range of drug, patient's ability (or lack of) to follow through with medication regimen and monitoring, and denial of need for information/therapy.

Sleep Pattern, disturbed: may be related to psychological stress, lack of recognition of fatigue/need to sleep, hyperactivity, possibly evidenced by denial of need to sleep, interrupted nighttime sleep, one or more nights without sleep, changes in behavior and performance, increasing irritability or restlessness, and dark circles under eyes.

Sensory/Perception, disturbed (specify) [overload]: may be related to decrease in sensory threshold, endogenous chemical alteration, psychological stress, sleep deprivation, possibly evidenced by increased distractibility and agitation, anxiety, disorientation, poor concentration, auditory/visual hallucination, bizarre thinking, and motor in-coordination.

Family Processes, interrupted: may be related to situational crises (illness, economics, change in roles); euphoric mood and grandiose ideas/actions of patient, manipulative behavior and limit-testing, patient's refusal to accept responsibility for own actions, possibly evidenced by statements of difficulty coping with situation, lack of adaptation to change or not dealing constructively with illness; ineffective family decision-making process, failure to send and to receive clear messages, and inappropriate boundary maintenance.

5. Forms

Mental Health Power of Attorney—Sample

AUTHORIZING INPATIENT PSYCHIATRIC CARE

I, _____ attest that
(Print your name)

when I cannot make my own mental health care treatment decision, I want all such decision to be made for me by my health care agent
_____ or, if I have appointed an alternate agent and my health care agent is unavailable or unwilling to serve, by my alternate health care agent
_____.

I want admission to a "level one behavioral health care facility" or "inpatient psychiatric hospital," if a physician determines that this is in my best interests, and agent agrees, at a time when I am unable to make my own mental health care treatment decisions, even if I oppose this.

_____
(Sign here in the presence of your witness)
Date: _____

STATEMENT OF WITNESS. I personally know the principle, and I believe him/her to be of sound mind and to have voluntarily (not under duress, fraud or undue influence) completed this health care power of attorney. I affirm that I am at least 18 years old, not related to him/her by blood, marriage or adoption, and not an agent named in this directive. I am not, to my knowledge, a beneficiary of his/her will or any codicil, and I have no claim against his/her estate. I am not directly involved in his/her health care.

_____
Witness Signature
Date: _____
Print witness name: _____
Phone: _____
Address: _____

Medical Records
Release Form

Date: _____

Attn: _____

RE: Release of Medical Records

Please release a copy of my medical/therapy records and prescription history to

_____

Once compiled, the records should be mailed to:

(Name) _____

(Address) _____

(City, State, Zip) _____

If you have any questions, you can reach me at (phone number): _____

Sincerely yours,

DBT: Is It for You?

Reprinted with permission from *Depressed & Anxious*
New Harbinger Publications, Inc. and Dr. Thomas Marra,
www.newharbinger.com

High Emotional Arousal	Yes	No
I feel tense, stressed, or on edge even when there is nothing immediately confronting me in the moment.		
I can't seem to relax as much as I would like to, even when I try.		
My hands shake or I'm anticipating failure a good deal of the time.		
I jump when a loud noise comes, even though I later find it wasn't anything dangerous.		
It takes me a lot longer than other people to relax.		
I'm always prepared or expecting something bad to happen to me.		
I feel vulnerable, like many things can hurt me, even though no one in particular is trying to hurt me.		
My emotions always seem to be "on" or prepared to be "on," even though I try to be calm and relaxed.		
I feel depressed.		
My feelings are intense, but I just can't get moving.		
Sometimes I just wish I would die.		
It doesn't take much to get me going (I react emotionally to even minor events).		
Many times "emotional" commercials make me cry.		
I wear my feelings on my sleeve in that, when I feel something, I typically express it openly.		
Other people tell me I'm an emotional person.		

	Yes	No
I believe I feel my emotions more intensely than others do		
When someone else hurts, I frequently hurt with him or her.		
I seem to be keyed in to what others are thinking and feeling.		
Slow Reduction in Emotional Tension	**Yes**	**No**
Once I feel an emotion, it's hard for me to stop feeling it.		
My strong emotions seem to last forever.		
I can't stop feeling anxious or depressed without great effort.		
Distrust of Emotions	**Yes**	**No**
My feelings frequently don't tell me how I should best behave or what to do next.		
I can't trust my gut reactions like others seem to be able to do.		
I wish I could eliminate my feelings, since they seem to get in my way rather than help me most of the time.		
Emotional Escape	**Yes**	**No**
When I feel tense, I do everything possible in order to feel differently as fast as possible.		
When someone hurts me, I immediately leave the room, usually no matter what the consequences or how it will look.		
When I begin to feel down or depressed, I can't stand it.		
I can't stand strong emotions, even if they are normal.		
Emotional Avoidance	**Yes**	**No**
I stay away from people who make me uncomfortable, even if they are not mean to me.		
I avoid situations and people who have hurt me in the past, even when this is difficult to do.		

	Yes	No
I do whatever I can to avoid being hurt, even though I may miss opportunities to get what I want in the future.		
People who know me well might call me a "fraidy cat" because I won't take chances.		
I'm afraid of my strong feelings.		

Sense of Urgency	Yes	No
I can't wait to solve my problems, even though I know it took a long time for the problems to develop.		
I would say I'm impulsive. I do things without a lot of thinking because I want quick results.		
People tell me I'm impatient because I want what I want *now*.		
I'm anxious because I feel that my problems are so bad they should be changed immediately. They are so bad that I can't wait for my problems to be solved.		
I feel dread about the future. Something bad is going to happen if I'm not careful.		
I frequently do things without thinking them through.		
I feel pressure to make changes in my life.		

Scoring

# of "Yes" Answers	IS DBT for You?
Fewer than 10	DBT is probably not for you.
11 to 15	DBT has something to offer you.
16 to 24	DBT is definitely for you.
More than 24	DBT is what you have been looking for, for a long time.

Mood Chart

Awareness is everything. By remaining mindful and aware of your feelings and those of the bipolar in your life, you are better able to identify, monitor and address triggers as they manifest themselves your life.

The chart on the following page is for everyone and is best used when combined with your journal and therapy, helping you to see patterns of behavior or reactions that might otherwise go unnoticed. The *patterns* that emerge may be helpful in adjusting medications or better identifying issues for therapy, so completing this chart will be very helpful to both your physician and therapist.

To use the list, simply fill in the box that best indicates your mood at the time and, if used by your spouse or partner, what they observe. Some of the things on the list will not apply to you; simply skip them and complete the ones that do apply to you and to how you are feeling.

This is a shortened list. For a more complete list you can go to www.meehlfoundation.org and download copies of the list as needed.

The Meehl Foundation

Mood Chart

	1 = mild	2 = moderate		3 = severe		4 = very severe	
Fatigue, lack of energy	0 0 0 0	0 0 0 0	0 0 0 0	0 0 0 0	0 0 0 0	0 0 0 0	0 0 0 0
Out of control, overwhelmed	0 0 0 0	0 0 0 0	0 0 0 0	0 0 0 0	0 0 0 0	0 0 0 0	0 0 0 0
Crying	0 0 0 0	0 0 0 0	0 0 0 0	0 0 0 0	0 0 0 0	0 0 0 0	0 0 0 0
Anxiety	0 0 0 0	0 0 0 0	0 0 0 0	0 0 0 0	0 0 0 0	0 0 0 0	0 0 0 0
Irritability	0 0 0 0	0 0 0 0	0 0 0 0	0 0 0 0	0 0 0 0	0 0 0 0	0 0 0 0
Feeling sad or blue	0 0 0 0	0 0 0 0	0 0 0 0	0 0 0 0	0 0 0 0	0 0 0 0	0 0 0 0
Insomia	0 0 0 0	0 0 0 0	0 0 0 0	0 0 0 0	0 0 0 0	0 0 0 0	0 0 0 0
Hypersomia	0 0 0 0	0 0 0 0	0 0 0 0	0 0 0 0	0 0 0 0	0 0 0 0	0 0 0 0
Confusion, difficulty concentrating	0 0 0 0	0 0 0 0	0 0 0 0	0 0 0 0	0 0 0 0	0 0 0 0	0 0 0 0
Aches	0 0 0 0	0 0 0 0	0 0 0 0	0 0 0 0	0 0 0 0	0 0 0 0	0 0 0 0
Arguments	0 0 0 0	0 0 0 0	0 0 0 0	0 0 0 0	0 0 0 0	0 0 0 0	0 0 0 0
Avoiding physical contact	0 0 0 0	0 0 0 0	0 0 0 0	0 0 0 0	0 0 0 0	0 0 0 0	0 0 0 0
Lonely	0 0 0 0	0 0 0 0	0 0 0 0	0 0 0 0	0 0 0 0	0 0 0 0	0 0 0 0
Boredom	0 0 0 0	0 0 0 0	0 0 0 0	0 0 0 0	0 0 0 0	0 0 0 0	0 0 0 0
Spending money	0 0 0 0	0 0 0 0	0 0 0 0	0 0 0 0	0 0 0 0	0 0 0 0	0 0 0 0
Grandiose ideas	0 0 0 0	0 0 0 0	0 0 0 0	0 0 0 0	0 0 0 0	0 0 0 0	0 0 0 0
Hypersexual	0 0 0 0	0 0 0 0	0 0 0 0	0 0 0 0	0 0 0 0	0 0 0 0	0 0 0 0
Missing days of work	0 0 0 0	0 0 0 0	0 0 0 0	0 0 0 0	0 0 0 0	0 0 0 0	0 0 0 0
Low self -esteem	0 0 0 0	0 0 0 0	0 0 0 0	0 0 0 0	0 0 0 0	0 0 0 0	0 0 0 0
Addicted: TV,computer, porn, drugs, alcohol	0 0 0 0	0 0 0 0	0 0 0 0	0 0 0 0	0 0 0 0	0 0 0 0	0 0 0 0
Housework done	0 0 0 0	0 0 0 0	0 0 0 0	0 0 0 0	0 0 0 0	0 0 0 0	0 0 0 0
Untalkative	0 0 0 0	0 0 0 0	0 0 0 0	0 0 0 0	0 0 0 0	0 0 0 0	0 0 0 0
Uncommunicative/unresponsive(incl. sex)	0 0 0 0	0 0 0 0	0 0 0 0	0 0 0 0	0 0 0 0	0 0 0 0	0 0 0 0
Unable to make decissions	0 0 0 0	0 0 0 0	0 0 0 0	0 0 0 0	0 0 0 0	0 0 0 0	0 0 0 0
Poor appetite or overeating	0 0 0 0	0 0 0 0	0 0 0 0	0 0 0 0	0 0 0 0	0 0 0 0	0 0 0 0
Self-absorbed	0 0 0 0	0 0 0 0	0 0 0 0	0 0 0 0	0 0 0 0	0 0 0 0	0 0 0 0
Demanding or critical	0 0 0 0	0 0 0 0	0 0 0 0	0 0 0 0	0 0 0 0	0 0 0 0	0 0 0 0
Raging	0 0 0 0	0 0 0 0	0 0 0 0	0 0 0 0	0 0 0 0	0 0 0 0	0 0 0 0
Physical violence	0 0 0 0	0 0 0 0	0 0 0 0	0 0 0 0	0 0 0 0	0 0 0 0	0 0 0 0
Unpredictable/changeable	0 0 0 0	0 0 0 0	0 0 0 0	0 0 0 0	0 0 0 0	0 0 0 0	0 0 0 0
Illogical or unreasonable	0 0 0 0	0 0 0 0	0 0 0 0	0 0 0 0	0 0 0 0	0 0 0 0	0 0 0 0
Manipulative	0 0 0 0	0 0 0 0	0 0 0 0	0 0 0 0	0 0 0 0	0 0 0 0	0 0 0 0
Pleasant in public/opposite at home	0 0 0 0	0 0 0 0	0 0 0 0	0 0 0 0	0 0 0 0	0 0 0 0	0 0 0 0
Refering to separation/divorce	0 0 0 0	0 0 0 0	0 0 0 0	0 0 0 0	0 0 0 0	0 0 0 0	0 0 0 0
Workaholism or avoidance of responsibility	0 0 0 0	0 0 0 0	0 0 0 0	0 0 0 0	0 0 0 0	0 0 0 0	0 0 0 0
Increased energy	0 0 0 0	0 0 0 0	0 0 0 0	0 0 0 0	0 0 0 0	0 0 0 0	0 0 0 0
Increased talking	0 0 0 0	0 0 0 0	0 0 0 0	0 0 0 0	0 0 0 0	0 0 0 0	0 0 0 0
Racing thoughts	0 0 0 0	0 0 0 0	0 0 0 0	0 0 0 0	0 0 0 0	0 0 0 0	0 0 0 0
Inappropriate elation	0 0 0 0	0 0 0 0	0 0 0 0	0 0 0 0	0 0 0 0	0 0 0 0	0 0 0 0
OCD	0 0 0 0	0 0 0 0	0 0 0 0	0 0 0 0	0 0 0 0	0 0 0 0	0 0 0 0
Demeaning others	0 0 0 0	0 0 0 0	0 0 0 0	0 0 0 0	0 0 0 0	0 0 0 0	0 0 0 0
Dating or bonding	0 0 0 0	0 0 0 0	0 0 0 0	0 0 0 0	0 0 0 0	0 0 0 0	0 0 0 0
Playing or having fun	0 0 0 0	0 0 0 0	0 0 0 0	0 0 0 0	0 0 0 0	0 0 0 0	0 0 0 0
Saw triggers	0 0 0 0	0 0 0 0	0 0 0 0	0 0 0 0	0 0 0 0	0 0 0 0	0 0 0 0
	0 0 0 0	0 0 0 0	0 0 0 0	0 0 0 0	0 0 0 0	0 0 0 0	0 0 0 0
	0 0 0 0	0 0 0 0	0 0 0 0	0 0 0 0	0 0 0 0	0 0 0 0	0 0 0 0
	0 0 0 0	0 0 0 0	0 0 0 0	0 0 0 0	0 0 0 0	0 0 0 0	0 0 0 0
	0 0 0 0	0 0 0 0	0 0 0 0	0 0 0 0	0 0 0 0	0 0 0 0	0 0 0 0

6. Free Medications

Many pharmaceutical manufacturing companies offer *Free Medications* for low income and disabled patients. Generally, you will find that your doctor has the necessary forms for you to complete.

As part of the process, your doctor must sign the application and attach a prescription to it and mail it directly to the pharmaceutical company.

On the following pages we have provided this information on the off chance your doctor or therapist is unaware of this program or you need to order the application yourself. You may download this information from www.bpphoenix.com or www.needymeds.com.

Abilify	**Bristol Myers Squibb Patient Assistance Program for Abilify**
	PO Box 8309
	Somerville, NJ 08876
	(800) 736-0003. option 1
Anafranil	**Mallinckrodt Patient Assistance Program**
	Pharmacy Providers of Oklahoma
	PO Box 18204
	Oklahoma City, OK 73154
	(800) 259-7765, ext.110
Aricept	**Pfizer Pharmaceuticals Aricept Assistance Program**
	1480 Arthur Avenue, Ste. D
	Louisville, CO 80027
	(800) 226-2072
Clozapine (generic)	**Ivax Pharmaceuticals Mylan Clozapine Patient Assistance Program**
	PO Box 4310
	Morgantown, WV 26504-1310
	(888) 823-7835
Clozaril	**Novartis Pharmaceuticals**
	Cozaril Patient Support Program
	(800) 257-3273, opt. 1
Concerta	**Janssen Pharmaceuticals Senior Patient Assistance Program**
	PO Box 221009
	Charlotte, NC 28222-1009
	(888) 294-2400
Depakote	**Abbott Laboratories Patient Assistance Program Pharmaceutical Products Div.**
	Dept D-13C, J23
	200 Abbott Park Rd.
	Abbott Park, IL 60064
	(800) 222-6885

Effexor	**Wyeth Pharmaceutical** **Patient Assistance Foundation** PO Box 1759 Paoli, PA 19301-0859 (800) 568-9938
Geodon	**Pfizer Pharmaceuticals** **Patient Assistance Program** PO Box 52119 Phoenix, AZ 85072 (866) 443-6366
Klonopin	**Roche Labs** **Patient Assistance Program** Medical Need Department Roche Laboratories 340 Kingsland St. Nutley, NJ 07110-1199 (800) 285-4484
Lamictal	**GlaxoSmithKline** **Bridges To Access** PO Box 29038 Phoenix, AZ 85038 (866) 728-4368
Lithium (generic)	**SmithKlineBeecham Foundation** **Access to Care** c/o Express Scripts/SDS PO Box 2564 Maryland Hts., MO 63043-8564 (800) 546-0420

Prozac	**Eli Lilly** **Lilly Cares** **Patient Assistance Program** PO Box 230999 Centerville, VA 20120 (800) 545-6962
Resperdal	**Janssen Pharmaceuticals** **Patient Assistance Program** PO Box 221098 Charlotte, NC 28222-1098 (800) 652-6227
Seroquel	**AstraZeneca Foundation** **Patient Assistance Program** PO Box 66551 St. Louis, MO 63166-6551 (800) 424-3727
Topamax	**Janssen Pharmaceuticals** **Senior Patient Assistance Program** PO Box 221009 Charlotte, NC 28222-1009 (888) 294-2400
Zoloft	**Pfizer, Inc.** **Pfizer Connection to Care** P.O. Box 66585 St. Louis, MO 63043-8564 (800) 707-8990
Zyprexa	**Eli Lilly** **Lilly Cares Patient Assistance Program** PO Box 230999 Centerville, VA 20120 (800) 545-6962

7. Things to Do Together

You need to get out together, spend time alone and reconnect. This doesn't have to cost a lot of money, it just takes time. Make the time and you will find that these moments together will lead to a more caring, nurturing and loving relationship for both of you. Here are 36 fun things you can do together (some much more fun than others—*but all fun*), and we're sure you can think of lots more.

1. Dinner out at a nice restaurant
2. Going to a concert
3. Spending the day at the beach
4. Rock climbing or mountaineering
5. Playing golf
6. Attending a sports event
7. Going to the races
8. Boating (canoeing, kayaking)
9. Camping
10. Going to church functions
11. Joining a social club
12. Dancing
13. Snow skiing
14. Taking a bath together
15. Playing board or card games together
16. Bowling
17. Sitting in the sun—together
18. Breathing deep in the mountains
19. Going to a museum or exhibit
20. Fishing
21. Eating at a drive-thru eatery (like McDonalds)
22. Horseback riding
23. Going to the movies
24. Kissing
25. Going to a restaurant
26. Playing computer games

27. Playing together, wrestling, tickling, laughing
28. Running, jogging, walking
29. Walking barefoot
30. Making a date for sex
31. Going on nature walks, even close to home
32. Having coffee with friends
33. Taking a vacation without the kids
34. Going to a Bed and Breakfast for the weekend
35. Lying in the sun
36. Taking a drive in the country

More things (up to you)

♦ _____

♦ _____

♦ _____

♦ _____

♦ _____

...and so on, and so on, and so on.

The
Meehl Foundation

The Meehl Foundation, located in Gilbert, Arizona, is focused on helping families, partners and friends of bipolars deal with Bipolar Disorder by providing information, resources and advice on how to deal with this illness.

We believe that it is possible not only to survive but also to thrive in a bipolar relationship by implementing agreements, changing perceptions and learning how to restructure the environment and individual responses and reactions so as to reduce triggers and the impact they have on everyone.

The focus of the Foundation is on teaching *Mindfulness*, *Emotional Stability* and *Personal Spirituality*, combined with medication and therapy, to reduce and overcome the affects of this illness. Through seminars and support groups, the Foundation helps bring sanity back into your life and teaches people how to create mutually supportive and caring environments, while living with Bipolar Disorder.

http://www.meehlfoundation.org

In its national speaking engagements, the Meehl Foundation teaches the **"The 6 Keys: Living with a**

Bipolar or Depressed Partner." This interactive presentation teaches participants how to:

- ♦ Understand the power and role of *mindfulness, meditation and affirmations.*
- ♦ Learn to *depersonalize* the actions of the bipolar.
- ♦ Develop skills to *reduce trigger*s and *create a mutually supportive relationship*.
- ♦ Bring more *balance* to your life by converting your reactions to responses.
- ♦ Steps to achieving *wellness* for yourself.
- ♦ *Develop boundaries* and *produce measurable results* in your relationship.

The Meehl Foundation's work is based on our living every day with Bipolar Disorder in our marriage and our home. We bring a real understanding of the challenges faced by partners, families and friends trying to live with this illness. We know that mental illness affects everyone, not just the person suffering from the illness. Understanding this, the Foundation provides people with real answers to their questions, and techniques that are proven, to help them live with Bipolar Disorder in their lives.

You can reach the Meehl Foundation through its website at www.meehlfoundation.org.

About the authors

Mark and Debra Meehl live in Arizona. Mark is bipolar and spends his days writing and working with Debra on the Meehl Foundation.

Debra divides her time between speaking engagements, writing, and working as a Life Coach.

This is their first book.

The couple is currently working on a companion book to the Survival Guide, ***The 6 Keys Manual: A 12-Month Guide for Bipolars and Families***, which is scheduled for publication in September, 2005 (see following page).

Available September, 2005

The 6 Keys Manual:
a 12-month guide for bipolars
and their families

The purpose of the *6-Keys Manual* is to help couples and family members learn to live with bipolar disorder by enabling them to take control over the emotional chaos that surrounds this upsetting and often confusing condition. This informative, educational, results-oriented program is structured as a workbook that takes both the non-bipolar and the bipolar partner on a 52-week, recovery-focused journey. Each week's installment is a distinct, very personal (and often introspective) topic-focused segment of the trip to wellness. Employing proven tools for emotional growth and physical control, the Manual covers every topic all couples, family members or bipolars need to consider and deal with in learning to live successfully—and even to thrive!—with Bipolar Disorder.

The *6-Keys Manual* was written with the understanding and compassion that comes only from the hands-on experience of living each day in a bipolar relationship. By following the weekly lessons, you will be able to re-create, nurture and build once again the committed, loving relationships that you deserve. These mutually supportive interactions, developed through feelings and appropriate actions, have been shown to produce growing, expanding relationships that can be enormously rewarding for both the non-bipolar and the bipolar (and their families and friends).

For more information or to order this life-enhancing program, go to http://www.meehlfoundation.org
or http://www.opapresents.com

LaVergne, TN USA
03 January 2011

210830LV00001B/109/A